YOUR recipe could appear in our next cookbook!

T0028184

Share your tried & true family favorites with us instantly at

www.gooseberrypatch.com

If you'd rather jot 'em down by hand, just mail this form to...

Gooseberry Patch • Cookbooks – Call for Recipes
PO Box 812 • Columbus, OH 43216-0812

If your recipe is selected for a book, you'll receive a FREE copy!

Please share only your original recipes or those that you have made your own over the years.

Recipe Name:

Number of Servings:

Any fond memories about this recipe? Special touches you like to add
or handy shortcuts?

Ingredients (include specific measurements):

Instructions (continue on back if needed):

Special Code: **cookbookspage**

Over ➴

Extra space for recipe if needed:

Tell us about yourself...

Your complete contact information is needed so that we can send you your FREE cookbook, if your recipe is published. Phone numbers and email addresses are kept private and will only be used if we have questions about your recipe.

Name:

Address:

City: State: Zip:

Email:

Daytime Phone:

Thank you! Vickie & JoAnn

Welcome
Autumn

A bounty of tasty recipes and ideas
for celebrating the season.

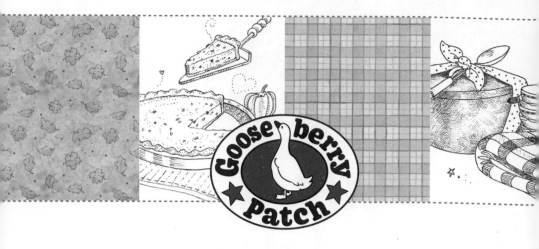

Gooseberry Patch

An imprint of Globe Pequot
64 South Main Street
Essex, CT 06426

www.gooseberrypatch.com

1•800•854•6673

Copyright 2023, Gooseberry Patch 978-1-62093-519-4

Do you have a tried & true recipe...

tip, craft or memory that you'd like to see featured in
a **Gooseberry Patch** cookbook? Visit our website at
www.gooseberrypatch.com and follow the
easy steps to submit your favorite family recipe.
Or send them to us at:

Gooseberry Patch
PO Box 812
Columbus, OH 43216-0812

Don't forget to include the number of servings your recipe makes,
plus your name, address, phone number and email address. If we
select your recipe, your name will appear right along with it...
and you'll receive a **FREE** copy of the book!

Contents

Dedication

If you love cheering at homecoming games, taking the kids to the pumpkin patch and cooking up all your favorite autumn recipes for family & friends, this book is for you.

Appreciation

Thanks to everyone who shared their very best recipes of the season.

Happy
Autumn
Memories

Welcome AUTUMN

A School Bus Cake

Doreen Evangelista
Peekskill, NY

My sons are now in their twenties, but I still make them a back-to-school bus cake. It's an idea I clipped out of a magazine back in the late 1990s, and it instantly became a neighborhood treat that took a little of the bittersweet sting out of the end of summer. It was simply two loaf cakes. One is cut a little shorter to become the body of the bus, which you cover with yellow frosting. Add some mini chocolate-covered doughnuts for wheels, decorate with red hots and white chocolate chips for lights, and some dark icing gel to write children's names or the name of their school on the side. Lots of wonderful memories are attached to this simple cake!

School days, school days,
Dear old Golden Rule days...

–Old song

Happy Autumn
Memories

Autumn Walks Home

Stefani Lynch
Cement, OK

Growing up, we had a long gravel driveway that wound through several acres of blackjack oak trees. Every day, we walked down that long driveway to get to the school bus and home again. Those walks that I took with my siblings home in the afternoons are some of my favorite memories. The bright colors of the leaves and the smells of the woods just made you feel like you were in the thick of the forest, with no one else around. It could also be a bit creepy at times, especially when we spotted some of the wildlife peeking back at us!

Magical Fall Colors

Kristian Stull
Myrtle Beach, SC

When I was a teen, I lived in a mountain village in North Carolina called Fontana Dam. In the fall, the bus ride to school would start out very dark. But a few minutes into the ride, the sun would come out over the mountain's trees to reveal the most beautiful mosaic of purples, reds, yellows and orange. I couldn't wait to ride to school each morning... it was magical!

A fallen leaf is nothing more than a summer's wave goodbye.
–Unknown

Welcome AUTUMN

Cutting Wood for Winter

Shirley Howie
Foxboro, MA

I grew up in Vermont on a small dairy farm and we lived in an old farmhouse that was built in 1852. We were kept busy from morning until night. There was always something to do to keep things running smoothly. One of the most memorable jobs we had was our wood-cutting operation, which took place every October. We had only a wood-burning furnace in the cellar, which heated the whole house, so it was necessary to ensure that we had enough wood to see us through the long, cold Vermont winters! I remember well those beautiful October days with bright blue skies, and the crisp autumn air that seemed to welcome us as we went into our woods to do our job. Mom would pack a picnic basket filled to the brim with sandwiches and her wonderful homemade cookies and cakes. Everything seemed to taste better outdoors! We would work all day, taking a break at lunchtime to enjoy all of Mom's goodies. When the trailer on Dad's tractor was filled, which was usually late afternoon, we would head for home. Then we had the job of throwing all the cut wood down the open hatch into the cellar, then stacking it all neatly in rows. The wood had to "cure" or dry out, so it would be used the following winter and we would use last year's wood for the upcoming winter. These memories have such a special place in my heart and remind me of a time long ago, when everything seemed right with the world!

Happy Autumn
Memories

Family Apple Orchard Trips

Sue Scott
Jackson, MI

My favorite childhood memory and activity was going apple picking. We would load up our old red pickup truck with bushel baskets and big plastic buckets and head to the family orchard of my stepdad's childhood friend. He would share stories of shenanigans in the orchard and ice skating on their pond in the winter. I would be the climber and get the apples high up in the tree. It was probably the most carefree and happiest time of year for me. I had the pleasure of getting to take my three sons with their PawPaw and Gramma a couple times before my mom passed, and it became a treasure for them as well. The smells of Mother's homemade applesauce and apple cake still fill my memory with a cozy amazing scent. I will forever cherish those days, that old truck and that special early autumn magical time with loved ones.

A Fall Potluck & Bonfire

Sandra Turner
Fayetteville, NC

Every year on the first Saturday in November, our church has a family potluck and bonfire. One of the families in our church lives in the country, and they open up their home and yard for this special event. The kids are treated to a hayride around the property, and we roast marshmallows, make s'mores and enjoy the crisp fall air. Although we see our friends at church each week, there is often little time to actually visit. I always look forward to catching up with them while enjoying the wonderful food. This is a great time of food, fellowship and fun.

Old-Time Halloween

Cindy Slawski
Medford Lakes, NJ

Halloween has always been a special and happy time of the year for me. My brother and I would start planning our costumes even before summer was over, and they were always homemade, which for me, made it even more fun. On the first of October, I would drag in our box of decorations from the garage and the house would be transformed into a creepy haunted mansion! When the long-awaited day finally came, my friends and I enjoyed all the school parties and parades, and even got a jump on trick-or-treating on our way home. But, nighttime would bring the most fun! We traversed the neighborhoods collecting full-size candy bars, quarters and other special treats, only stopping to eat a quick dinner of hot soup and grilled cheese and to touch up our make-up. When it finally got too late to trick-or-treat, my brother and I would return home, spread our goodies out on the floor and commence trading, while sampling a candy or two. Though I am in my 50s now, these Halloween memories are still so vivid and truly some of my happiest!

When black cats prowl and pumpkins gleam,
May luck be yours on Halloween.
–Old rhyme

Happy Autumn
Memories

Celebrating Fall

Helen McKay
Edmond, OK

Fall has always been my favorite season. The days are getting cooler and nights may bring frost. It reminds me of harvesting our family garden, and helping my mom with canning all the vegetables and fruit to eat during the winter months. And so many more memories...raking leaves into big piles and jumping into them, or making leaf houses. Getting excited for Halloween and planning with my friend our route for trick-or-treating! As I've gotten older, now married with kids and grandkids, fall continues to bring me all these memories and more. When my kids were young, I started the tradition of a fall dinner to celebrate the beginning of the season. Roast turkey, potatoes, various squashes, warm homemade rolls and Mom's apple crisp for dessert. Our family looks forward to bringing in the fall season with this special meal. It's a beautiful time of year!

Sing a song of seasons,
Something bright in fall!
Flowers in the summer,
Fires in the fall!

–Robert Louis Stevenson

An Apple-Scented Memory

Sara Tatham
Plymouth, NH

When I was growing up, one of the things my family always did in fall was to visit a local orchard to pick up our order of apple "drops." There was a favorite orchard, called Rockledge Orchard, where my parents always purchased apples. In our family lexicon it was abbreviated simply to "Rockledge." Mention that and everyone knew what was meant. To get there, one took a network of dirt roads, following the homemade signs. To the best of my knowledge, we didn't ever pick up the "drops" off the the ground ourselves. Instead, my mother would order a bushel or two of "Macs" and Cortlands. The orchard folks would fill these large wooden boxes with apples that had dropped to the ground. This meant, of course, that the apples weren't perfect, but they were fine for our purposes and they were less expensive. And what a treat it was to go to the orchard to pick up our apple order! The boxes of apples were stored in a large room in the barn, to keep them cool and in good condition. Oh, the aroma inside that barn! It was a lot like Yankee Candle's McIntosh scent, only better, of course. Every single time I smell that scent, it takes me back. But the aroma in that barn was even better! When we got our apples home, my mother made lots of applesauce to can, and I'm sure she made some apple crisps and apple squares as well (she wasn't much of a pie baker) but many of the apples were just to eat out of hand. The Cortlands, with their bright red outsides and crunchy white flesh, were my very favorites. The apples and the treats made from them were marvelous...but they just can't compare to the sweetness of that apple-scented memory!

Happy Autumn
Memories

Apple Day Cider Pressing

Jessica Stubbs
Forney, TX

My family had "Apple Day" every fall. My grandparents had an apple press, and we would make fresh-pressed cider and bob for apples. My aunt and uncle continue the tradition with pressing cider and making homemade applesauce in a giant copper pot over a fire. It's so much fun just getting the entire family together, and nothing says it's fall like a mug of fresh cider!

An Autumn Visitor

Allie Rockwell
Harrisburg, PA

My favorite memory is from a day years ago. It was a beautiful, sunny, quiet fall day in beautiful Oak Ridge, New Jersey. I thought I heard something outside. I looked outside from the back door, and there was a beautiful, magnificent white-tail doe, taking her time eating acorns that had fallen to the ground from a tall oak. I had forgotten that memory until now. Thanks for helping me remember that precious time in my life.

Welcome AUTUMN

Making Leaf Houses

Susan Johnson
Bloomington, MN

Back in the 1950s when I was young, my family's home had seven very large oak trees in the front yard. Of course, a lot of time was spent raking all those leaves! But my mom and older sister taught me something else to do with them. We raked the leaves into the outlines of houses, leaving openings for doors and hallways, a lot like a blueprint outline looks. After creating our new house, my friends and I would spend many hours "playing house," adding some props from home...small chairs, a little table, dolls, etc. Our imaginations went wild as we played. The best part of doing this is now sharing this activity with my two young granddaughters. We started a few years ago. They look forward to our October visits, when we "build" leaf houses together. They make a garage and park their wagon and Little Tykes cars, as well as making a bedroom for each of them. We move the plastic kitchen "inside," and they're all set for a great afternoon. To get ready, my husband moves all the maple leaves before he mows the grass, so that we'll have enough leaves for the houses. Oh my, such fun we've had!

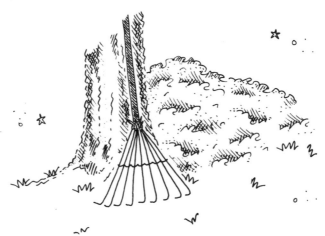

October's the month when the smallest breeze
Gives us a shower of autumn leaves.
Bonfires and pumpkins, leaves sailing down...
October is red and golden and brown.

–Unknown

Happy Autumn
Memories

Fall Colors in Arizona

Lillie Reed
Wonder Lake, IL

I have a special memory of growing up in Phoenix, Arizona and the time my parents decided we all needed to see the fall colors up north. We all packed up in the car and drove up through Oak Creek Canyon and Sedona to see the beautiful fall colors. It was breathtaking! I remember the air was crisp and cool, so different from how it was in the desert. We stopped by a roadside stand in Oak Creek Canyon and picked up a bag of fresh-picked apples. Those were the sweetest apples I had ever tasted. That memory is so special to me that I made sure my own kids could have that memory too. We live in northern Illinois and we go apple picking every September. They have grown up with this tradition and a few years ago, we added a new generation...my five-month-old granddaughter was going as well!

Fall Memories from Arkansas

Beckie Apple
Grannis, AR

Growing up in rural Arkansas as a young girl, I have such fond memories of the simple life our farm family lived. My brothers and sisters and I loved to be outdoors all summer, but we especially looked forward to fall and the simple joys that it brought. Hayrides were always one event we really loved. Our Uncle Bill would load up the haywagon with fresh hay and take all the kids in our small community for a hayride. We knew what awaited us at the end of the ride...a hot dog and marshmallow roast over a big campfire, mugs of hot chocolate and best of all, watermelons from his own patch. I will always treasure those wonderful memories. Life was so good back then!

Autumn Walnut Picking

Patricia Addison
Cave Junction, OR

When I was growing up, fall was a very exciting time to look forward to. My birthday was in the fall, along with my two most favorite holidays, Halloween and Thanksgiving. But the best part of fall for me was my little business of selling walnuts. Every fall, I went around the neighborhood and gathered several large sacks of walnuts in my wagon. I would be walking my dog at the same time...and trust me, she was very little help! She would see a walnut and assume it was a toy for her, so she stole walnuts from the sacks as we walked along on our route. On weekends, I went over to a neighbor's place, where he had a half-acre of walnut trees that he helped me pick to sell. I would take the walnuts home and lay them out to dry on old screen doors. Then as the husks dried, I would crack them. My customers had a choice of shelled walnuts or walnuts in the shell for their holiday baking, a dollar a bag. This was my favorite activity during the fall and that was how I earned my Christmas money each year. My neighbors loved this, as my nut prices were a lot cheaper than the stores and I had plenty of nuts to supply them with. Dad thought this was a good way for me to earn money, too. He helped by setting up sawhorses to lay two screens across to let the husks dry evenly. I loved his help and I loved my business. Mom had walnuts for her chocolate chip-nut cookies and walnut bread for our fall treats. All that walking got me in great shape for Halloween night, too! We would walk up and down five or six blocks for treats. It was a good time, and I wish I could do it all again one more time.

Happy Autumn
Memories

Preceding Winter

Jaki Browne
Conway, NH

To me, autumn has always been an indicator of winter being just around the corner. The images of bare trees, brisk cold and freezing snow, would on occasion invade my enjoyment of fall. To quash those thoughts of winter, my sisters and I as young children would rake leaves and make a huge pile of leaves. Then we'd run and jump into the pile of leaves, and hide. We'd completely cover ourselves with leaves and wait until someone, usually our mother, would walk past and one or all three of us would jump out of the pile. Mother would pretend to be startled. We believed she was actually frightened, which in turn caused us to laugh and jump around in the leaves. After playing in the leaves for awhile, we'd create a scarecrow stuffed with some of the leaves, which was always a fun project for us. These memories bring me back to a time of innocence, laughter and special times with my siblings.

The leaves fall, the wind blows, and the farm country
slowly changes from the summer cottons
into its winter wools.

–Henry Beston

Costumes Made with Love

Karla Himpelmann
Mount Pleasant, MI

Back in the 1980s, I tried to be a creative mom. I would make Halloween costumes for my two children. I didn't buy anything to make the costumes, I just used whatever I found around the house and in their box of too-small clothes. I came up with some clever ideas for Shari and Kevin. It was such fun piecing their costumes together! I did a lot of sewing different pieces of fabrics together to come up with whatever popular characters everyone wanted to be that year. I made spider costumes, the Queen of Hearts, a grouch in a garbage can. There were endless ideas that I put together with their help. On Halloween, when it came time to wear their costumes, the children always looked wonderful and happy in the costumes their mom had made for them with love.

Trick-or-Treating

Jacki Smith
Fayetteville, NC

Every year on Halloween, we would come right home from work and school, then make Sloppy Joes and French fries to eat before heading out to trick-or-treat. When we returned home after trick-or-treating, we would gather at the kitchen table to inspect the night's haul. Once all the candy and treats had been inspected, the trading began. Even our parents ended the night sampling the treats! Peanut butter cups and peppermint patties were always big favorites at our house. The tradition continues on with the grandchildren.

Happy Autumn
Memories

A Vampire Dinner

Monica Britt
Fairdale, WV

Each Halloween, my nieces and nephews come to trick-or-treat at my house last, because we have a "Vampire Dinner." It has become such a much-anticipated tradition. I set the table with mood-setting items such as a red tablecloth and black candlesticks, and dim the lights. Placeholders are vampire teeth with name cards. The menu changes from year to year, but stays true to the theme. Anything goes, from spooky spiderweb pizza to mummy hot dogs and red velvet cupcakes. It's such a wonderful time to sit around the table together on a cool fall night after trick-or-treating and listen to their stories!

Halloween Haunted Orchestra

Lisa Staib
Tumbling Shoals, AR

One of our Colorado homes had a huge front yard with one enormous oak tree. Each year, I decorated the porch and yard for all holidays. But one fall, I wound up with three metal band music stands! My daughters played in pep band. So, with headless musicians, black-painted broken chairs and instruments and a black spiderweb blowing in the tree, I created a Haunted Orchestra. During Halloween week, I played haunted music in the yard...ah-ooooo!

Family Thanksgiving

Cindy Winfield
Nacogdoches, TX

When I was growing up, every Thanksgiving was spent at my grandparents' house. It was always an exciting day as the women gathered in the kitchen early to start preparing our traditional Thanksgiving meal. My sister and I had the job of buttering the rolls and helping set the table. There was so much talking and laughing going on in that small kitchen as my mother, grandmother and aunt worked like clockwork, each with her own part in preparing our special meal. When it was finally time to eat, we would all gather around the table in the dining room and enjoy our meal together. As our family grew, we added more chairs to that table, which became a little crowded, but that was fine...it just meant more laughter and love.

Over the river and through the wood
trot fast, my dapple gray!
Spring over the ground like a hunting hound,
for this is Thanksgiving Day.

–L. Maria Child

Happy Autumn
Memories

Grandmother's Home Cooking

Anita Polizzi
Bakersville, NC

My grandmother made almost everything from scratch. She cooked everyday, sometimes three meals a day. On Saturday night, she fried hamburgers in a cast-iron frying pan. She would pour her home-canned tomato juice over them and let them simmer...they were so good! In the fall and winter, we would make homemade fudge in that cast-iron pan. The recipe came from a cookbook she had gotten when they bought a "Home Comfort" brand wood stove. I have her cookbook, and it is one of my prized possessions. To make sure the candy had come to the correct soft-ball stage, she would drop a little in a cup of cold water. She would let me eat it off her finger. Nothing ever tasted any better! She taught me how to cook, and how to put love in everything that you cook.

If you werc to ask me what is most important
in a home, I would say memorics.
–Lillian Gish

A Hawaiian Thanksgiving

Kathy Neuppert Swanson
Hemet, CA

In the early 1970s, my brother Tim attended college in Redlands, California, and had the fortune of meeting many classmates from the Hawaiian Islands there. One year, we learned that a group of them were unable to fly home for the Thanksgiving holiday. Our sweet mom agreed to host them all for a turkey dinner with all the trimmings. I eagerly jumped right in by cleaning the house, borrowing a neighbor's metal beverage cooler and learning to make Hawaiian sweet potatoes. Yum...they were the hit of the dinner! As late afternoon turned into evening, we all sat cracking nuts out of their shells and enjoying pumpkin pie. To our delight, it turned out that our guests were not only students, but amazing musicians. They played guitars and sang "Tiny Bubbles" and "Yellow Bird" for our entertainment. It was heartwarming to see my brother so happy with his family & friends gathered that day...my favorite Thanksgiving memory, for sure!

Recall it as often as you wish...a happy memory
never wears out!

–Libbie Fudim

Busy-Day
Breakfasts

Welcome AUTUMN

Pumpkin-Chocolate Chip Pancakes

Donna Wilson
Maryville, TN

There is nothing like the smell of sweet pumpkin pancakes in the morning to bring everyone together! Adding chocolate chips makes it an extra treat.

2-1/2 c. pancake mix
1-1/4 c. milk or buttermilk
1 egg, beaten
1/2 c. canned pumpkin
2 T. brown sugar, packed

1/4 c. butter, melted
1-1/2 t. pumpkin pie spice
1/2 c. mini semi-sweet
   chocolate chips
Garnish: butter, pancake syrup

In a large bowl, combine all ingredients except chocolate chips and garnish. Stir together until combined; fold in chocolate chips. Lightly grease a griddle; heat over medium heat. Scoop batter onto griddle by 1/3 cupfuls. Cook until bubbles form on top; flip over and cook the other side. Serve with butter and syrup. Makes about one dozen.

On a sunny autumn morning, take your coffee out
to the front porch...enjoy nature's beauty and
wave to neighbors passing by!

Busy-Day
Breakfasts

Upside-Down Cranberry-Pecan Cinnamon Rolls

Marsha Baker
Pioneer, OH

I so love the ease of dressing up canned biscuits. These taste like they came straight from the bakery. They're extra special for the holidays. Don't miss this recipe...enjoy every fabulous bite!

1/4 c. butter, melted
1/4 c. brown sugar
1/4 c. dried cranberries

1/4 c. chopped pecans
13-oz. tube refrigerated
  cinnamon rolls

In a small bowl, mix together melted butter and brown sugar. Spread in the bottom of an ungreased 9" round cake pan; sprinkle with cranberries and pecans. Arrange rolls evenly in pan; set aside icing package. Bake at 375 degrees for 20 to 23 minutes, until lightly golden. Remove from oven. Turn pan upside-down onto a large serving plate; do not remove pan. Let stand for about 5 minutes before removing. Scrape any brown sugar mixture remaining in pan over rolls. Stir reserved icing and drizzle or spoon over rolls. Makes 8 servings.

Send kids off to school with a breakfast they'll love...waffle sandwiches. Tuck scrambled eggs, a browned sausage patty and a slice of cheese between a pair of waffles. Yum!

Maple Sausage Breakfast Casserole

Ellen Folkman
Crystal Beach, FL

I created this tasty recipe using the last few croissants I had on hand. It's a great make-ahead dish for any occasion, since it's refrigerated overnight before baking.

2 T. butter, melted
3 large croissants, cubed
1/2 lb. ground pork sausage
1/4 c. sweet onion, chopped

2 T. pure maple syrup
1/2 c. shredded Cheddar cheese
4 eggs, beaten
1 c. half-and-half

Brush melted butter on the bottom and sides of a 9"x9" baking pan. Add croissant cubes to pan; set aside. Brown sausage with onion in a skillet over medium heat; drain. Reduce heat to medium-low. Stir in maple syrup; mix well and remove from heat. Spoon sausage mixture over croissant cubes; sprinkle with cheese. In a bowl, blend together eggs and half-and-half; spoon over croissant mixture. Cover and chill for 8 hours or overnight. When ready to bake, uncover pan. Bake at 350 degrees for 40 to 45 minutes, until egg mixture is set and croissants are golden. Serves 4 to 6.

Bring friends & neighbors together for a casual brunch...if it's a warm day, you can even hold it outdoors. Welcome them with steaming mugs of hot cider or coffee and tea. Serve favorite foods buffet–style...what a fun way to enjoy each other's company!

Busy-Day
Breakfasts

Ham & Hashbrown Casserole

Doug Shockley
Lincoln, NE

I make this delicious casserole for a monthly men's breakfast I attend, and the men have continued to ask for it. Put it together the night before, bake the next morning...easy!

2 28-oz. pkgs. frozen diced
   hashbrown potatoes, thawed
1 lb. cooked ham, diced
1 to 2 8-oz. pkgs. shredded
   Cheddar cheese, divided

Optional: diced onions,
   diced green pepper
1 doz. eggs, beaten
1 to 2 c. milk
salt and pepper to taste

In a large bowl, combine potatoes, ham and one package shredded cheese; add onions and green peppers, if using. Mix well; transfer to a deep 13"x9" baking pan coated with non-stick vegetable spray. In the same bowl, whisk together eggs and milk. Season with salt and pepper; pour over potato mixture. Cover and refrigerate overnight. Uncover; bake at 350 degrees for one to 1-1/2 hours. If desired, top with remaining package of shredded cheese; return to oven just until melted. Serves 8 to 10.

Oven-Baked Omelet

Coleen Lambert
Luxemburg, WI

Just such an easy recipe and so good. It's special to me, because my grandkids help me make it before they go to bed. They just love it! It's all about making memories with the girls.

8 eggs, beaten
1/2 c. half-and-half
1 c. shredded Cheddar cheese
1 c. cooked ham, chopped

1/4 c. red and/or green
   peppers, diced
1/4 c. onion, minced

In a large bowl, whisk together eggs and half-and-half until light and fluffy. Stir in remaining ingredients; pour into a greased 9"x9" baking pan. Bake, uncovered, at 400 degrees for 25 minutes, or until set. Cut into squares. Makes 4 servings.

Spicy Taco Breakfast Burritos

Andie Dietz
Portage, MI

Whenever I travel, I leave a stash of frozen burritos for my husband, more than he should need while I'm away. When I return, every last burrito is gone...I think he eats them for every meal! Use my special taco seasoning mix or the storebought kind.

1 lb. ground pork breakfast
    sausage
Optional: diced tomatoes,
    peppers and/or onions
1 to 2 T. taco seasoning mix
2 T. water

1 doz. eggs, beaten
pepper to taste
8 8-inch flour tortillas
8 slices American cheese
taco sauce, salsa or hot pepper
    sauce to taste

Brown sausage in a large skillet over medium heat, adding optional vegetables, if using. Drain; stir in seasoning mix and water. Simmer until water evaporates. In a large bowl, whisk together eggs and pepper. Add to sausage in skillet; cook and stir over medium heat until eggs are set. On a microwave-safe plate, stack tortillas with damp paper towels in between. Microwave tortillas for 30 seconds. Divide eggs among warmed tortillas. Top with cheese and sauce; roll up, tucking in sides. Makes 8 burritos.

Homemade Taco Seasoning Mix:

2 T. chili powder
1 T. ground cumin
2 t. cornstarch
2 t. salt

1-1/2 t. hot smoked paprika
1-1/2 t. ground coriander
1/2 t. cayenne pepper

Combine all ingredients in a glass jar. Cover and shake well; store up to 6 months. To use, add one to 2 tablespoons to one pound of meat.

Paper coffee filters make tidy
holders for breakfast burritos.

Busy-Day *Breakfasts*

Carol's Maple Sausage Breakfast Patties

Carol Kiermaier
Benton, PA

I didn't care for commercial breakfast sausage, so I worked on developing one we would like. This version is my husband's favorite...adjust it for your family's seasoning preferences.

1-1/2 lbs. ground pork
1 T. pure maple syrup
1 t. dried sage
1/4 t. dried thyme
1/4 t. dried marjoram

1/8 t. red pepper flakes
1/8 t. ground cloves
1/8 t. allspice
1 t. salt
3/4 t. pepper

Place pork in a large bowl; drizzle with maple syrup and set aside. In a small bowl, mix remaining ingredients; sprinkle over pork. Mix to distribute seasonings well. Form into uniform small patties. Cook patties in a skillet over medium-low heat until golden and no longer pink in the center. Patties may be formed, wrapped uncooked and frozen for future use. Makes 6 to 8 servings.

Make a scrumptious apple topping for pancakes and waffles. Sauté 3 cups sliced apples in a tablespoon of butter over medium-high heat until tender, about 8 minutes. Stir in 1/4 cup maple syrup and sprinkle with 1/2 teaspoon cinnamon. Serve warm.

Welcome AUTUMN

Golden Harvest Muffins

Janis Parr
Ontario, Canada

I have made these scrumptious muffins so many times and we never get tired of them. They are moist and full of flavor, and are a great way to get some fruit and vegetables into the kids. These muffins freeze well...but really, there are never any left at our house!

1 c. all-purpose flour
1 c. whole-wheat flour
1 c. sugar
2 t. baking soda
2-1/4 t. cinnamon
1/4 t. ground cloves
1/2 t. salt
2 c. McIntosh apples, peeled, cored and shredded

1/2 c. carrot, peeled and shredded
1/2 c. flaked coconut
1/2 c. golden raisins
1/2 c. chopped pecans
3/4 c. oil
1/4 c. milk
2 eggs, beaten
2 t. vanilla extract

In a large bowl, combine flours, sugar, baking soda, spices and salt; mix well. Stir in apples, carrot, coconut, raisins and pecans. Add oil, milk, eggs and vanilla; stir just until combined. Spoon batter into 18 greased muffin cups, filling 3/4 full. Bake at 350 degrees for 20 to 25 minutes, until a toothpick inserted in the center comes out clean. Immediately remove muffins from pan; serve warm. Makes 1-1/2 dozen.

After a hearty breakfast, pack a picnic lunch and hop in the car. Take a favorite route to see the fall color, or go down that country lane you've always wondered about...who knows where it will lead?

30

Busy-Day
Breakfasts

Fried Apple-Maple Rings

Patricia Addison
Cave Junction, OR

This is a perfect fall breakfast for those chilly weekend mornings.
Really delicious! If you can't find apple-cinnamon pancake mix,
combine one cup biscuit baking mix and 2 teaspoons apple pie spice.

1 c. apple-cinnamon pancake mix
1 c. milk
1 egg, beaten
1 T. butter, melted
1 t. vanilla extract
2 t. oil or butter
2 firm apples, peeled, cored and
  cut into 1/4-inch rings
Garnish: additional butter,
  maple syrup

In a bowl, combine pancake mix, milk, egg, butter and vanilla. Mix until just blended; batter will be a bit lumpy. Heat skillet over medium heat; brush with oil or butter. Dip each apple slice into batter; add to skillet. Cook for one to 2 minutes per side, until golden. Serve hot with plenty of butter and maple syrup. Serves 4.

Mix up some yummy honey-pecan spread for toasted bagels!
Combine a softened 8-ounce package of cream cheese with
2 tablespoons honey and beat until smooth. Fold in 1/2 cup
toasted chopped pecans. Chill before serving.

Back-to-School Cheesy Bacon & Egg Muffins

Christina Burrell
North Richland Hills, TX

With five precious children, this recipe is a quick and healthy favorite at our house on early-morning school days. I bake a double batch on the weekend, freeze them and then reheat as needed each morning. I love that they are portable, on-the-go portions we can take in the car if we're running late, and it gives me reassurance that my children have a healthy start to their day.

10 thin slices turkey bacon
10 eggs, beaten
1/2 c. milk
1/4 t. dry mustard
1 t. salt
1/4 t. pepper
Optional: 1/8 t. red pepper flakes

2 c. frozen shredded hashbrown
   potatoes
3/4 c. finely shredded Cheddar
   cheese
3/4 c. finely shredded mozzarella
   cheese

In a large skillet over medium heat, cook bacon until crisp. Drain; remove bacon to paper towels. Meanwhile, in a bowl, beat together eggs, milk and seasonings; set aside. Crumble bacon and divide evenly among 12 greased or paper-lined muffin cups; top with potatoes. Pour egg mixture evenly into muffin cups; top with cheeses. Bake at 350 degrees for 20 to 25 minutes, until eggs are no longer jiggly in the center. Let muffins cool slightly before serving. Makes one dozen.

To freeze: Let cool; wrap in aluminum foil and freeze in a plastic freezer bag. To serve, unwrap desired number of muffins. Place on a microwave-safe plate; microwave for 45 seconds to one minute.

A quick fall craft for kids...hot glue large acorn caps onto round magnets for whimsical fridge magnets.

Busy-Day
Breakfasts

Banana-Caramel Monkey Bread
Michelle Newlin
Portage, PA

*A wonderful way to wake up the family. Sometimes we add
a handful of walnuts...scrumptious!*

1 firm banana, sliced
1/4 c. sugar
1/2 c. brown sugar, packed
　and divided

16.3-oz. tube refrigerated sweet
　Hawaiian biscuits, cut into
　quarters
6 T. butter, melted

Coat a 12-cup fluted tube cake pan with non-stick baking spray. Arrange
sliced bananas in the bottom of pan in a single layer; set aside. In a
large plastic zipping bag, mix sugar and 1/4 cup brown sugar. Add
biscuit pieces to bag; shake in bag to coat. Layer biscuits in pan. In a
small bowl, combine remaining brown sugar with any sugar mixture left
in bag. Mix in melted butter; spoon over biscuits. Bake at 350 degrees
for 30 to 35 minutes, until baked through and deeply golden. Cool in
pan 5 minutes. Turn pan upside-down onto a serving plate; serve
warm. Makes 8 servings.

Keep a tin of pumpkin pie spice on hand to jazz up pancakes,
muffins and coffee cakes. A quick shake adds cinnamon,
nutmeg and allspice all at once.

Crustless Spinach-Green Chile Quiche

Jenna Harmon
Dolores, CO

When I have visitors, I always make this quiche with fresh spinach from my garden, and now it is everyone's favorite! I make this with almond flour so my gluten-free family members can enjoy it also.

1/4 c. all-purpose or almond flour	1 c. shredded Pepper Jack cheese
1/2 t. baking powder	1 c. small-curd cottage cheese
1/2 t. salt	1-1/4 c. fresh spinach, chopped
6 eggs	4-oz. can chopped green chiles
	1/4 c. butter, melted

In a large bowl, whisk together flour, baking powder and salt; set aside. In another bowl, beat eggs until smooth. Whisk in flour mixture until all lumps are gone. Stir in remaining ingredients until blended; pour into a greased 8"x8" baking pan. Bake, uncovered, at 400 degrees for 15 minutes. Reduce oven to 350 degrees. Bake for an additional 40 minutes, or until a knife tip inserted in the center comes out clean. Cut into squares. Serves 6.

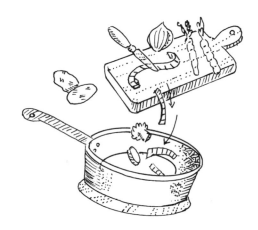

Egg dishes are a perfect way to use up tasty tidbits from the fridge...baked ham, crispy bacon and chopped veggies. Warm briefly in a skillet and set aside for an omelet filling, or scramble the eggs right in.

Busy-Day
Breakfasts

Broken Breakfast Burrito

Caroline Britt
Cleveland, TX

Whenever I used corn tortillas in this dish, they broke because they weren't very pliable. That's how this broken burrito dish was created, by turning something broken into something amazing.

1/2 lb. bacon, crisply cooked
   and crumbled
2 to 3 T. canola oil
5 10-inch corn tortillas,
   cut into strips
1 onion, chopped

1 green pepper, chopped
2 to 3 bunches green onions,
   chopped
1 doz. eggs, beaten
1/4 c. evaporated milk
1 c. shredded Cheddar cheese

In a large skillet over medium heat, cook bacon until crisp. Set aside bacon to drain on paper towels. Drain skillet; add oil and heat over medium heat. Add tortillas and vegetables; sauté until tender. Meanwhile, whisk together eggs and evaporated milk. Add egg mixture and crumbled bacon to skillet; scramble together until cooked through. Top with shredded cheese; let stand until melted. Makes 10 to 12 servings.

Biscuit & Gravy Bake

Penny Sherman
Ava, MO

A great hearty breakfast before a busy Saturday! For a crowd, double the recipe and use a deep 13x9 baking pan.

1 lb. ground pork breakfast
   sausage
3 T. butter
1/4 c. all-purpose flour

2-1/2 c. milk
salt and pepper to taste
16-oz. tube refrigerated biscuits,
   cut into quarters

Brown sausage in a skillet over medium heat; set aside sausage on paper towels. Drain skillet, reserving one tablespoon drippings in skillet. Melt butter in skillet. Sprinkle with flour; stir until blended. Cook until flour is golden, about 2 minutes. Whisk in milk; cook and stir for 2 to 5 minutes, until thickened. Season generously with salt and pepper. Return sausage to skillet; mix well. Spread sausage mixture in a greased 9"x9" baking pan; arrange biscuit pieces on top. Bake, uncovered, at 350 degrees for 22 to 24 minutes, until biscuits are golden. Serves 6.

Welcome AUTUMN

Cheesy Sausage-Muffin Bake

Vickie
Gooseberry Patch

Easy to put together for breakfast meetings at work, tailgating, you name it! Sometimes I'll spice it up with Pepper Jack cheese.

1/2 lb. ground pork breakfast
    sausage
8 English muffins, cut into
    6 pieces, divided
1-1/2 c. shredded Cheddar
    cheese, divided

5 eggs, beaten
1-1/4 c. milk
1-1/2 t. salt
1/2 t. pepper

Brown sausage in a skillet over medium heat; drain well. Spread half of English muffin pieces evenly in a greased 8"x8" baking pan. Layer with half each of sausage and cheese. Repeat layering; set aside. In a bowl, whisk together remaining ingredients; spoon evenly on top. Cover and refrigerate for 2 hours or overnight. Uncover; bake at 325 degrees for 40 to 50 minutes, until center is set. Let cool for 5 minutes; cut into squares and serve. Makes 4 to 6 servings.

Easy Egg Muffins

Caroline Britt
Cleveland, TX

This is an easy breakfast for little ones and adults alike. It can be wrapped and tucked in the fridge, too...easy to reheat, grab & go!

6 eggs
8-oz. pkg. real bacon bits

1 c. shredded Cheddar cheese
6 English muffins, split

Spray 6 muffin cups with non-stick vegetable spray. Crack one egg into each cup; top with bacon bits and cheese. Bake at 350 degrees for 20 minutes, or until centers are set. Place each egg in an English muffin and serve. Makes 6 sandwiches.

I'm so glad I live in a world where there are Octobers.

-Lucy M. Montgomery

Busy-Day
Breakfasts

B&B Egg Roll-Up

Stephanie Nilsen
Fremont, NE

We first tasted this at a bed & breakfast in Iowa. It's all the regular breakfast ingredients, but served up so prettily, it makes breakfast time special!

4 T. butter, melted and divided
1/4 c. all-purpose flour
1 doz. eggs, beaten
1 c. cottage cheese
1/3 c. whipping cream
1 t. salt-free seasoning
1 lb. ground pork breakfast
   sausage

8-oz. pkg. shredded Cheddar
   cheese
1/2 c. red or green salsa
Garnish: additional shredded
   cheese, salsa

Line a 15"x10" jelly-roll pan with parchment paper; spread one tablespoon melted butter over paper and set aside. In a large bowl, mix together remaining butter and flour. Beat in eggs, cottage cheese, cream and seasoning, either by hand or using a food processor. Spread mixture in pan. Bake at 350 degrees for 20 minutes, or until set. Meanwhile, brown sausage in a skillet over medium heat; drain and set aside. Remove pan from oven. Sprinkle with shredded cheese; drizzle with salsa and crumble sausage over all. Starting on one long edge, roll up jelly-roll style, using the parchment paper as you roll. Place roll on a serving platter; garnish as desired. Slice and serve. Serves 8 to 10.

Whip up some special hot cocoa with a round disc of Mexican chocolate...it has the sugar and cinnamon already mixed in. Bring 4 cups milk almost to a boil, add the chopped chocolate and whisk until it's melted and creamy.

37

Janet's Best Granola

Janet Reinhart
Columbia, IL

Loving granola, I've collected many recipes, combining and tweaking until I came up with my favorite. I love this topped with an equal amount of cottage cheese, while my husband prefers vanilla yogurt with his. We often also split a chopped peach or apple between our bowls. Yum!

3 c. old-fashioned oats, uncooked
1/2 c. dry-roasted peanuts
1/2 c. chopped almonds
1/3 c. pepitas or pumpkin seeds
3/4 c. unsweetened flaked coconut
1/4 c. flax seed meal
1/4 c. coconut oil

2 T. brown sugar, packed
2 T. honey
2 T. agave nectar or honey
1 T. vanilla extract
2 t. cinnamon
1/8 t. salt
1/4 c. dried cranberries
1/4 c. dried blueberries
1/4 c. dried mango, chopped

In a large bowl, combine oats, nuts, pepitas, coconut and flax seed meal; stir well and set aside. In a microwave-safe 2-cup glass measuring cup, combine coconut oil, brown sugar, honey, agave nectar, vanilla, cinnamon and salt. Microwave cup for 30 seconds, or until oil is melted and brown sugar is dissolved. Stir well. Pour warmed oil mixture over oat mixture; stir until well coated. Spread oat mixture evenly into a thin layer on 2 parchment paper-lined baking sheets. Set baking sheets on 2 oven racks. Bake at 325 degrees for 25 minutes, stirring after 10 minutes and swapping oven racks, again after 20 minutes and on removing from oven. Allow to cool on stovetop; sprinkle with dried fruit. Store granola in a large airtight container; serve in 1/4-cup to 1/2-cup portions. Makes 16 to 24 servings.

Scoop homemade granola into easy-to-tote sports bottles...ideal for snacking when you're out & about to fall festivals and flea markets.

Busy-Day
Breakfasts

Strawberry-Oatmeal Breakfast Smoothies

*Joyceann Dreibelbis
Wooster, OH*

This is a fast and filling smoothie with a rich, creamy texture and a deep pink color. A great quick and healthy breakfast!

1/2 c. rolled oats, uncooked
1 c. soy milk or whole milk
1 ripe banana, cut into chunks

14 frozen strawberries, hulled
1/2 t. vanilla extract
1 t. sugar

If desired for a smoother texture, process oats in a blender. Add soy milk, banana and strawberries to oats in blender; process until fruit is chopped. Add vanilla and sugar; blend until smooth. Pour into 2 glasses and serve. Makes 2 servings.

A hollowed-out pumpkin makes a fun flower vase...try other hard winter squashes too! Cut an opening at the top of the squash and slip in a small plastic cup or square of floral foam. Fill with flowers and add water to keep them fresh.

Welcome AUTUMN

Mom's Breakfast Doughnuts

Vickie Wiseman
Liberty Township, OH

My mom was making these doughnuts as far back as I can remember, and I was born in 1953. My brothers and sister all loved them...I hope you will, too!

3-1/2 c. all-purpose flour
1 T. baking powder
3/4 t. salt
1 t. cinnamon
1/2 t. nutmeg
1/2 c. shortening, melted and
    slightly cooled

1/3 c. milk
4 eggs, beaten
2/3 c. sugar
oil for deep frying
Garnish: cinnamon-sugar and/or
    powdered sugar

In a bowl, combine flour, baking powder, salt and spices; set aside. In another bowl, combine melted shortening and milk. In a large bowl, combine eggs and sugar; beat with electric mixer on medium speed until thick, about 5 minutes. Add milk mixture to eggs; stir with a wooden spoon to combine. Add flour mixture and stir until smooth. Cover and chill for 2 hours; dough will remain slightly sticky. Turn dough out onto a lightly floured surface. Roll out dough to 1/2-inch thickness. Cut dough with a floured 2-1/2 inch round cutter; cut out centers with a 1-1/4 inch cutter. (Or, use a doughnut cutter, if you have one.) Heat several inches oil in a heavy saucepan over medium-high heat to 375 degrees. Add 2 to 3 doughnuts and doughnut holes; fry for 2 to 2-1/2 minutes until golden, turning halfway through with a slotted spoon. Drain on paper towels. Repeat with remaining doughnuts and doughnut holes. Shake warm doughnuts in a bag with cinnamon-sugar and/or powdered sugar; serve warm. Makes about 15 doughnuts and doughnut holes.

Cinnamon-sugar is scrumptious on all kinds of breakfast items. In a small jar, mix together 1/2 cup sugar and one teaspoon cinnamon. Seal jar and keep in a cool, dry place.

Busy-Day
Breakfasts

Ultimate French Toast Deluxe

Karen McCann
Marion, OH

I developed this recipe from one I found several years ago in a magazine. I added some ingredients and perfected it to my own liking...it made this French toast like no other. It is delicious...enjoy!

2 eggs, beaten
1/4 c. milk
1-1/2 c. frosted corn flake cereal, crushed
1 T. toasted flaked coconut

Optional: 1 T. chopped pecans or walnuts
6 slices Texas toast, 1-inch thick
oil for frying

In a shallow dish, whisk together eggs and milk until well blended; set aside. Place crushed cereal in another shallow dish; add coconut and nuts, if using. Dip each slice of Texas toast into egg mixture and roll in cereal mixture, coating well. Add oil to coat the bottom of a large skillet; heat over medium to medium-high heat. Add toast slices to hot oil, a few at a time. Cook on both sides until golden, turning once; turning more often will cause crumb mixture to fall off. Serve warm. Makes 6 servings.

Boiled cider is a terrific topping for pancakes or oatmeal... desserts too. It's simple to make. Pour 2 quarts apple cider into a heavy saucepan. Bring to a boil, then reduce heat and simmer gently for 1-3/4 hours, until cider has boiled down to 1-1/2 cups. Cool; refrigerate in a wide-mouth jar.

Cinnamon Roll Poke Cake

Rita Morgan
Pueblo, CO

Just add a breakfast casserole and a pot of hot coffee...
a delicious breakfast is served!

15-1/4 oz. pkg. white cake mix
3 eggs, beaten
1 c. water
1/2 c. oil
6 T. plus 2 t. sweetened
  condensed milk

5 T. butter, melted
1/2 c. brown sugar, packed
2 t. cinnamon
Garnish: favorite cream cheese
  frosting, additional cinnamon

In a large bowl, with an electric mixer on medium speed, beat together dry cake mix, eggs, water and oil until smooth. Pour batter evenly into a greased 13"x9" baking pan. Bake at 350 degrees for 29 to 33 minutes, until a toothpick tests clean. Set pan on a wire rack; cool completely. Meanwhile, in another bowl, whisk together condensed milk, melted butter, brown sugar and cinnamon until smooth; set aside. With the handle of a wooden spoon, poke holes all over cooled cake. Pour condensed milk mixture into the holes. Spread cake with frosting; sprinkle with a little cinnamon. Cut into squares and serve. Makes 10 to 12 servings.

Serve fuss-free favorites like Cinnamon Roll Poke Cake...
ideal for tailgating Saturday morning. Everyone can easily
help themselves while the day's fun is beginning.

Busy-Day
Breakfasts

Easy Overnight Breakfast Bake

Denise Webb
Bloomingdale, GA

My daughter's best friend shared this recipe with me. The seasoned croutons add a great taste and texture to this dish.

1-1/2 to 2 lbs. ground pork
   breakfast sausage
5-oz. pkg. seasoned croutons
8-oz. pkg. shredded Cheddar
   cheese

4 eggs, beaten
2-1/2 c. milk, divided
3/4 t. dry mustard
10-3/4 oz. can cream of
   mushroom soup

Brown sausage in a large skillet over medium heat; drain well. Spread croutons in a greased 13"x9" baking pan. Top with sausage and cheese; set aside. In a large bowl, beat eggs, 2 cups milk and mustard; pour over cheese. Cover and refrigerate overnight. In the morning, whisk together soup and remaining milk; spoon over casserole. Bake, uncovered, at 300 degrees for 1-1/2 hours, or until set and golden. Makes 8 to 12 servings.

On Thanksgiving morning, serve fuss-free favorites like a breakfast casserole and a basket of muffins...ideal for overnight guests.

Sausage & Cheese Grits Quiche

Joan Chance
Houston, TX

*I enjoy this unusual recipe. Sometimes I sprinkle it with
freshly shredded Parmesan cheese at serving time.*

3 c. whole milk
1/4 c. butter
3/4 c. old-fashioned grits,
  uncooked
1 t. salt, divided
1/2 t. pepper, divided
1 c. shredded sharp Cheddar
  cheese
1 c. pasteurized process
  cheese, diced

6 eggs, beaten
1 c. whipping cream
1 T. Dijon mustard
1/2 lb. mild ground pork
  breakfast sausage, browned
  and drained
1/4 c. green onions, thinly sliced
Garnish: snipped fresh chives

In a large saucepan over medium-high heat, combine milk and butter.
Bring to a simmer for 5 to 7 minutes, stirring occasionally. Stir in grits,
1/2 teaspoon salt and 1/4 teaspoon pepper. Cook, stirring often, for
about 15 minutes, until mixture is thickened and grits are tender.
Remove from heat; stir in cheeses until smooth. Pour mixture into a
lightly greased 9" round springform pan. Let cool to room temperature,
about 30 minutes. Cover loosely with aluminum foil; chill for 8 to
24 hours. Set pan on a foil-lined rimmed baking sheet. In a large bowl,
whisk together eggs, cream, mustard and remaining salt and pepper.
Fold in sausage and onions; spoon evenly over grits mixture. Bake at
325 degrees for one hour and 10 minutes, or just until set. Let stand
for 20 minutes. At serving time, sprinkle with chives; cut into wedges.
Serves 10.

Fall is sweater weather...hang an
old-fashioned peg rack inside the
back door so everyone knows
just where to find their
favorite snuggly sweater!

Busy-Day
Breakfasts

Cheddar Sausage Biscuits

Shirley Howie
Foxboro, MA

These savory biscuits are wonderful for breakfast, brunch or lunch. They freeze well too. Let them cool completely, freeze them on a baking sheet and transfer to a freezer bag. I like to have some made up ahead for a quick breakfast on busy mornings!

1 lb. ground pork breakfast
    sausage, browned, drained
    and crumbled
3 c. biscuit baking mix

8-oz. pkg. shredded Cheddar
    cheese
1-1/2 c. milk

In a large bowl, combine all ingredients; mix until well blended. Drop mixture by tablespoonfuls onto a parchment paper-lined baking sheet. Bake at 450 degrees for 8 to 12 minutes, until golden. Makes about 1-1/2 dozen.

Dressed-Up Bacon

Paula Marchesi
Auburn, PA

Easy and delicious...once you taste this bacon, you may never go back to the plain kind! Great for football tailgating. Instead of walnuts, you can use pecans, hazelnuts or cashews. To spice it up a bit, sprinkle with a little pepper, chili powder or Cajun seasoning after adding the nut mixture.

12 thick-cut slices bacon
1/4 c. dark brown sugar, packed

1/2 c. walnuts, finely chopped
1 t. all-purpose flour

Arrange bacon slices on a greased broiler pan; set aside. In a small bowl, combine remaining ingredients. Sprinkle over bacon. Bake at 350 degrees for 25 to 30 minutes, until crisp and golden. Drain on paper towels. Makes 12 slices.

Breakfast Turkey Stack

Vickie Wiseman
Liberty Township, OH

This is a delicious meal! You can serve it on biscuits, English muffins or croissants, or even enjoy it by itself. I love the flavor of the sausage with the maple syrup added.

1 lb. ground turkey
4 t. pure maple syrup
1/2 t. dried sage
1/4 t. cayenne pepper
1/8 t. ground ginger
1/4 t. salt
1/8 t. pepper

1 t. olive oil
1 large ripe beefsteak tomato,
   cut into 4 slices
4 slices Cheddar cheese
Optional: biscuits, English
   muffins or croissants, split

Combine turkey, maple syrup and seasonings in a bowl; mix well. Divide into 4 patties, each 1/2-inch thick. Heat oil in a large non-stick skillet over medium-high heat. Cook patties until well-browned and cooked through, about 4 minutes per side. Remove from heat; set aside. Arrange tomato slices on an ungreased rimmed baking sheet in a single layer; season with additional salt and pepper. Top each tomato slice with one turkey patty and one cheese slice. Place under broiler until cheese is melted, about 2 minutes. Serve hot. Makes 4 servings.

Simple farmhouse-style table decorations are often the most charming! Fill a rustic wooden bowl with shiny red apples or scented pine cones for the kitchen table.

Busy-Day
Breakfasts

Apple-Raisin Oatmeal

Melody Taynor
Everett, WA

Love our Washington apples! This is a sweet, hearty breakfast, waiting for you in the morning. Serve topped with a splash of cream, if you like.

3-1/2 c. milk
1 Granny Smith apple, peeled,
   cored and diced
3/4 c. steel-cut oats, uncooked
3/4 c. golden raisins
3 T. brown sugar, packed

4-1/2 t. butter, melted
3/4 t. cinnamon
1/2 t. salt
1/4 c. chopped pecans
Optional: additional milk

In a lightly greased 3-quart slow cooker, combine all ingredients except nuts and optional milk. Cover and cook on low setting for 7 to 8 hours, until liquid is absorbed. Spoon oatmeal into bowls; top with pecans and milk, if desired. Makes 6 servings.

October's the month when the smallest breeze
Gives us a shower of autumn leaves.
Bonfires and pumpkins, leaves sailing down...
October is red and golden and brown.
     –Unknown

Jump-Start Banana Muffins

Courtney Stultz
Weir, KS

A classic banana-nut muffin is a perfect baked treat, but sometimes you just need to change things up a bit. These simple muffins add a bit of coffee to our favorite recipe to give them an extra kick! The coffee flavor is just enough for taste, but not too overpowering. They freeze well too.

3 large ripe bananas, mashed
2/3 c. oil
2 eggs, beaten
1 c. sugar
3 c. all-purpose or gluten-free
    flour

4 t. baking soda
3 t. cinnamon, divided
1 t. salt
3 T. instant coffee granules
1 c. chopped walnuts
3 T. brown sugar, packed

In a large bowl, combine bananas, oil, eggs and sugar; mix until combined. Add flour, baking soda, 2 teaspoons cinnamon, salt and coffee granules. Mix until just combined; fold in nuts. Scoop batter into 18 greased or paper-lined muffin cups, filling 2/3 full. In a cup, combine brown sugar and remaining cinnamon; sprinkle over batter. Bake at 350 degrees for about 18 to 20 minutes, until a toothpick inserted in center comes out clean. Remove muffins from pan; cool on a wire rack for about 10 minutes. Makes 1-1/2 dozen.

Such a neighborly gesture...invite the family of your child's new school friend over for a weekend brunch. Send them home with a basket filled with maps and coupons to local shops and attractions.

Busy-Day
Breakfasts

Mini Cinnamon-Sugar Muffins

Ellen Folkman
Crystal Beach, FL

I made these mini muffins all the time when my kids were little...they were perfect for tiny hands. Now I include them on my holiday brunch buffets.

5 T. butter, softened	2-1/4 t. baking powder
1/2 c. sugar	1/4 t. salt
1 egg, beaten	1/4 t. nutmeg
1/2 c. milk	Garnish: melted butter,
1-1/2 c. all-purpose flour	cinnamon-sugar

In a bowl, beat softened butter and sugar until light and fluffy. Add egg; mix well. Beat in milk. In another bowl, combine flour, baking powder, salt and nutmeg; add to butter mixture and beat until just moistened. Spoon batter into greased mini muffin cups, filling 2/3 full. Bake at 350 degrees for 14 to 16 minutes, until a toothpick comes out clean. Cool in pan for 5 minutes; remove muffins from pan to a wire rack. Dip muffins into melted butter; roll in cinnamon-sugar and serve warm. Makes 2 dozen.

Linen tea towels are oh-so handy in the kitchen. They're reusable too...much thriftier than paper towels! Look for vintage tea towels at tag sales, or dress up plain towels by stitching on brightly colored rick rack..

Welcome AUTUMN

Buttermilk & Cinnamon Waffles

Marie Smulski
Lyons, IL

These waffles are so fluffy and light, they melt in your mouth! Serve with fresh fruit and plenty of maple syrup for a wonderful meal.

2 c. all-purpose flour
1 T. brown sugar, packed
2-1/4 t. baking powder
3/4 t. cinnamon

1/4 t. salt
1-1/2 c. buttermilk
2 eggs, beaten
1-1/2 T. butter, melted

In a small bowl, whisk together flour, brown sugar, baking powder, cinnamon and salt. Make a well in the center. Add buttermilk, eggs and melted butter; stir just until combined. Pour batter by 1/4 cupfuls onto a preheated greased waffle maker; bake according to manufacturer's directions. Makes 8 to 10 waffles.

Asher's Favorite Pancakes

Elizabeth Conroy-Powers
Rochester Hills, MI

One day, my grandson wanted pancakes for lunch. I had sour cream on the counter...he dumped it in! The pancakes turned out great. I always double this recipe, as all my grandbabies love them.

1 egg, beaten
1 c. milk. or more as needed
3 T. butter, melted and
    slightly cooled
1/2 c. sour cream
2 c. all-purpose flour

3 T. sugar
2 t. baking powder
1 t. baking soda
1/4 t. salt
1 t. cinnamon
1 t. almond extract

In a large bowl, whisk together egg, milk, melted butter and sour cream. Stir in remaining ingredients, but do not overmix. Heat a greased griddle over medium-high heat. Add batter, 1/4 cup per pancake. Cook until golden on both sides. Makes 6 pancakes.

Busy-Day
Breakfasts

Skillet-Fried Cinnamon Apples

Tina Butler
Royse City, TX

*These Southern-fried apples are a simple, down-home side dish
that pair perfectly with any country meal or breakfast.*

1/4 c. butter
6 Granny Smith or Golden
   Delicious apples, peeled,
   cored and sliced
2 to 3 t. lemon juice
1/4 c. light brown sugar, packed

1/4 c. sugar
2 t. cinnamon
1-1/2 t. cornstarch
1/4 c. water
1/2 t. vanilla extract

In a large cast-iron skillet, melt butter over medium heat. Add apples
and sprinkle with lemon juice; sauté for 2 to 3 minutes. In a small bowl,
blend together sugars, cinnamon and cornstarch. Sprinkle over apples
and stir to combine, making sure all apples are fully coated. Stir in water
and vanilla; reduce heat to medium-low. Simmer apples for another
12 minutes, or until apples are fork-tender and cinnamon syrup in
skillet has thickened. Serve warm. Makes 6 servings.

Watch for old-fashioned syrup pitchers at tag sales...set out
a variety of sweet toppings like fruit-flavored syrups and
honey for pancakes and waffles.

Welcome AUTUMN

Cinnamon-Pecan Popovers

*Shirley Howie
Foxboro, MA*

This is a favorite Sunday morning breakfast. We like to try different kinds of jam, but a drizzle of warm maple syrup is our favorite. Make sure the oven is fully preheated and don't open the oven door to peek during baking!

1 c. milk
3 eggs, beaten
3 T. butter, melted and
   cooled slightly
1 c. all-purpose flour

1 t. cinnamon
1/4 t. salt
1/2 c. pecans, finely chopped
Garnish: butter, maple syrup
   or jam

Generously grease 8, 6-ounce custard cups; arrange on a baking sheet and set aside. In a blender, combine milk, eggs, melted butter, flour, cinnamon and salt. Process for 30 seconds to blend; do not overmix. Spoon batter into custard cups, filling about 1/3 full. Sprinkle tops with pecans. Bake at 400 degrees for 30 minutes, or until tops are golden. Turn popovers out of custard cups. Serve immediately, topped with butter and warm maple syrup or jam. Makes 8 popovers.

Make a simple fabric liner for a basket of fresh-baked muffins.
Use pinking shears to cut a large square of cotton fabric in
a sweet fall print. So easy...why not make one for the
breakfast table and an extra for gift-giving?

Harvest
Sides & Salads

Spectacular Overnight Salad

Carolyn Deckard
Bedford, IN

I can't remember which of my aunts used to make this crisp slaw
for our family fish fry at my uncle's cabin on the river. It goes
very well with fried fish and cornbread...keeps well too.

1 head cabbage, shredded
3/4 c. red onion, thinly sliced
1/2 c. green pepper, chopped
1/2 c. red pepper, chopped
1/2 c. green olives with
   pimentos, sliced
1/2 c. white wine vinegar

1/2 c. oil
1/2 c. sugar
2 t. Dijon mustard
1 t. mustard seed
1 t. celery seed
1 t. salt

In a large bowl, combine cabbage, onion, peppers and olives; set aside.
In a saucepan, combine remaining ingredients; bring to a boil over
medium-high heat. Cook and stir for one minute; pour over vegetables
and stir gently. Cover and refrigerate overnight. Stir well before serving.
Serves 12 to 16.

A vintage wooden salad bowl is a terrific thrift-shop find.
To restore the bowl's glowing finish, sand lightly inside and
out with fine sandpaper. Rub a little vegetable oil over the
bowl and let stand overnight, then wipe off any excess oil
in the morning. It will look like new!

Harvest
Sides & Salads

Best Macaroni Salad

Sarah Slaven
Strunk, KY

This is my favorite macaroni salad...it is so tasty! It's perfect for potlucks, as it's easy to put together.

12-oz. pkg. elbow macaroni,
   uncooked
4 eggs, hard-boiled, peeled
   and diced
1 orange pepper, chopped
1 red pepper, chopped
1/2 c. sweet onion, chopped

2 stalks celery, chopped
2 c. mayonnaise
1/4 c. sugar
3 T. mustard
2 T. dill pickle relish
2 t. white vinegar

Cook macaroni according to package directions; drain. Rinse in cold water; drain and transfer to a large bowl. Add eggs and vegetables; mix gently and set aside. In a small bowl, mix together remaining ingredients. Pour over macaroni mixture; toss to coat well. Cover and refrigerate at least one hour before serving. Makes 10 servings.

Give favorite pasta recipes a twist for fall...pick up some pasta in seasonal shapes like autumn leaves, pumpkins or turkeys! Some even come in veggie colors like orange, red or green.

Crunchy Pear & Celery Salad

Regina Wickline
Pebble Beach, CA

A crisp salad I love to serve in fall! If I'm making it ahead,
I add the pecans just before serving.

4 stalks celery, trimmed
   and halved lengthwise
2 T. cider vinegar
2 T. honey
1/4 t. salt
2 ripe Bartlett pears, cored
   and diced

1/2 c. Cheddar cheese,
   finely diced
1/2 c. chopped pecans, toasted
coarse pepper to taste
Optional: 6 leaves lettuce

Add celery to a bowl of ice water; let stand for 15 minutes. Drain well
and pat dry. Cut celery into 1/2-inch pieces; set aside. In a large bowl,
whisk together vinegar, honey and salt until well blended. Add pears;
stir gently to coat. Add celery, cheese and pecans; stir to combine.
Season with pepper. Serve at room temperature or chilled, spooned
onto lettuce leaves if desired. Makes 6 servings.

Toasting really brings out the flavor of chopped nuts. Add nuts
to a small dry skillet. Cook and stir over medium-low heat
for 2 to 4 minutes, until toasty and golden.

Harvest
Sides & Salads

Cranberry Waldorf Salad

JoAnn
Gooseberry Patch

This take on the traditional Waldorf salad has the added tartness
of dried cranberries. Try it with almonds instead of walnuts too!

2 c. Granny Smith apples, cored
   and chopped
2 c. Red Delicious apples, cored
   and chopped
juice of 3 lemons
1/2 c. celery, chopped

1/2 c. chopped walnuts
1 c. sweetened dried cranberries
1/2 c. grapes, halved
1 c. whipping cream
1/2 c. mayonnaise
1/8 t. nutmeg

In a large bowl, combine apples, lemon juice, celery, walnuts, cranberries and grapes; toss to mix and set aside. In a deep bowl, beat cream with an electric mixer on high speed until soft peaks form. Fold in mayonnaise; add to apple mixture and mix well. Sprinkle with nutmeg; cover and chill until serving time. Serves 8.

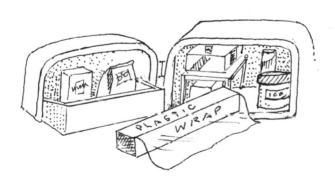

A little secret for plastic wrap...store the box in the freezer!
When used, it doesn't stick to itself, yet adheres well when
used to wrap food.

Cheesy Potatoes

Beckie Langford
Tappahannock, VA

These potatoes are always a hit at my house! They're a favorite for me too, because they are very easy to make.

28-oz. pkg. frozen diced potatoes
   & onions, thawed
10-3/4 oz. can cream of
   chicken soup
1/4 c. mayonnaise
1/4 c. sour cream
1 t. mustard

1/4 t. dried thyme
1/4 t. garlic powder
1/4 t. salt
1/4 t. pepper
8-oz. pkg. shredded Cheddar
   cheese, divided

In a large bowl, mix together all ingredients, reserving one cup Cheddar cheese for topping. Spoon mixture into a greased 9"x9" baking pan. Top with reserved cheese. Cover and bake at 350 degrees for 40 minutes. Uncover; bake for another 10 to 15 minutes, until bubbly and cheese is completely melted. Makes 6 servings.

For a quick & easy table runner, choose seasonal cotton fabric printed with autumn leaves and Indian corn in glowing gold, orange and brown. Simply pink the edges...it will dress up the dinner table all season long.

Harvest
Sides & Salads

Savory Mashed Sweet Potatoes

Karen Antonides
Gahanna, OH

This holiday recipe is a nice change from the traditional sweet-tasting sweet potato recipes. It's always well received at family dinners.

6 to 7 sweet potatoes, peeled
    and cut into 1-inch cubes
2 t. salt, divided
coarse pepper to taste
1 clove garlic, minced
1/3 c. green onions, finely sliced
    and divided

3 T. butter, cubed
4 T. sour cream, divided
1/3 c. fresh flat-leaf parsley,
    finely chopped

In a large saucepan, cover sweet potatoes with water; add one teaspoon salt. Bring to a boil over medium-high heat. Reduce heat to medium. Simmer, uncovered, for 9 to 12 minutes, until fork-tender. Drain potatoes well; transfer to a large bowl and mash to desired consistency. Stir in remaining salt, pepper, garlic and most of the onions. Add butter and 3 tablespoons sour cream; mix well. Transfer to a serving bowl; garnish with remaining sour cream, onions and parsley. Serves 6.

Put away summer toss pillows for the season...set out warm and cozy cushions of flannel or fleece.

Welcome AUTUMN

Southern Cornbread Dressing

Charlene McCain
Bakersfield, CA

My mother was famous for her dressing and passed this recipe on to me. It is a great dish at Thanksgiving. I like to serve it on other occasions as well, when I'm needing a little comfort-food fix.

4 T. butter, melted and divided
2 c. onions, diced
1/2 c. celery, chopped
3 c. biscuits or toasted bread, crumbled
1 T. dried sage

2 t. poultry seasoning
1/2 t. dried thyme
salt and pepper to taste
1 egg, beaten
3 c. chicken broth, heated

Bake Cornbread ahead of time; let cool. Coat a 13"x9" baking pan with 2 tablespoons melted butter; set aside. Add remaining butter to a skillet over medium heat. Cook onions and celery until tender and translucent. Transfer onion mixture to a large bowl. Mix in 3 cups crumbled Cornbread, biscuits or toast and seasonings; stir in egg. In a saucepan over high heat, bring chicken broth to a boil. Slowly pour 2-1/2 to 3 cups hot broth over mixture, stirring until moistened. Spoon mixture into pan. Bake, uncovered, at 350 degrees for about 30 minutes, until golden. Serves 10 to 12.

Cornbread:

1/3 c. plus 1 T. oil, divided
1 c. yellow cornmeal
1 c. all-purpose flour
1 T. baking powder

1-1/2 t. salt
1 egg, lightly beaten
1 c. buttermilk

Coat a 13"x9" baking pan with one tablespoon oil; set aside. Combine cornmeal, flour, baking powder and salt; set aside. In another bowl, whisk together egg, buttermilk and remaining oil. Gradually add egg mixture to cornmeal mixture; stir until moistened. Pour into pan. Bake at 400 degrees for 20 to 25 minutes, until a knife tip comes out clean.

Harvest
Sides & Salads

Green Bean Special

Kathy Rusert
Mena, AR

*My grandkids ask for this instead of the traditional
green bean casserole. I sometimes add red pepper
for a dish with seasonal colors.*

3 slices bacon
1/2 c. onion, chopped
1 green pepper, sliced
1 clove garlic, minced

2 lbs. green beans, trimmed
1 c. chicken broth
salt and pepper to taste

In a skillet over medium heat, cook bacon until crisp. Remove bacon
to a paper towel to drain. To drippings in skillet, add onion, pepper and
garlic. Cook for 5 minutes, or until onion is translucent. Add green
beans and chicken broth. Simmer for about 20 minutes, until liquid
evaporates and onion begins to caramelize. Season with salt and pepper;
top with crumbled bacon and serve. Serves 6.

Corn Pudding

Becky Orange
Maryville, TN

*My daughter said, "This is so good, you should make it instead of
dressing at Thanksgiving!" And, it's a small world...my name is
Becky Orange and I have a pen pal named Beckie Apple, who's a
fellow **Gooseberry Patch** contributor.*

15-1/4 oz. can corn, drained
15-oz. can cream-style corn
8-1/2 oz. pkg. cornbread mix

1/2 c. sour cream
1/2 c. butter, softened
3 eggs, beaten

In a large bowl, mix together all ingredients until moistened. Pour
batter into a well-greased 13"x9" baking pan. Bake at 400 degrees
for 45 minutes, or until golden. Cut into squares. Makes 10 servings.

Tex-Mex Pasta Salad

Tracee Cummins
Georgetown, TX

My family loves this fresh salad! The dressing has just the right amount of kick to spice up any meal. This salad has been the star of many barbecues through the years!

12-oz. pkg. tri-colored corkscrew pasta, uncooked
1 c. mayonnaise or salad dressing
1/2 c. Italian salad dressing
4-oz. can chopped green chiles, partially drained
1 t. chili powder
1 t. ground cumin
15-1/2 oz. can red kidney beans, drained
15-oz. can corn, drained
1 to 2 ripe tomatoes, chopped
1/2 c. green pepper, chopped

Cook pasta as package directs; drain and rinse with cold water until completely cool. In a large salad bowl, blend mayonnaise, salad dressing, chiles and seasonings. Add pasta and remaining ingredients; toss to coat well. Cover and chill until serving time. Makes 6 to 8 servings.

Pick any late-blooming herbs in the garden and tuck the stems into a welcoming grapevine wreath for the front door. They'll dry naturally, keeping their sweet and spicy scents.

Harvest
Sides & Salads

Bean, Rice & Feta Salad

Nancy Putnam
Lake Stevens, WA

Easy, tasty and simple...one of my favorites!

15-1/2 oz. can black beans,
    drained and rinsed
1-1/2 c. ripe tomatoes, chopped
1-1/2 c. cooked rice, chilled
3-1/2 oz. pkg. crumbled
    feta cheese

1/2 c. celery, chopped
1/2 c. green onions, chopped
1/2 c. light Italian salad dressing
2 T. fresh cilantro, chopped, or
    more to taste

Combine all ingredients in a large bowl; mix well. Cover and refrigerate for at least 2 hours. Serve chilled. Makes 8 servings.

Frank's Corn Salad

Becky Butler
Keller, TX

I got this yummy recipe from a family friend, Frank. He always made it when he barbecued for our Scout troop. It's fabulous! I like to mix cans of yellow and white corn.

4 15-oz. cans corn, well drained
1/2 c. sweet onion, finely
    chopped
1 to 1-1/2 c. mayonnaise

1-1/2 c. shredded Cheddar
    cheese
9-1/4 oz. pkg. chili-cheese corn
    chips, crushed

In a large bowl, combine corn, onion and one cup mayonnaise; mix well. Cover and refrigerate for at least 2 hours. Just before serving time, add cheese and mix well. If mixture appears too dry, add a little more mayonnaise. Stir in crushed chips and serve. Makes 8 to 10 servings.

There is always something for which to be thankful.
–Charles Dickens

Country Cabbage

Melissa Dommert
Baytown, TX

This dish is so comforting on a chilly day. What may seem like a huge pile of cabbage will shrink down quite a bit as it cooks. The little bit of water added helps to steam the cabbage and the apple adds just a touch of sweetness.

3 to 4 slices bacon
1/2 c. onion, finely chopped
1/2 c. apple, cored and finely chopped
1 head cabbage, quartered and thinly sliced

1/2 t. Creole seasoning
salt and pepper to taste
1/2 c. water
Optional: 1 t. butter

Cook bacon in a large saucepan over medium heat until crisp. Remove bacon to a paper towel, reserving drippings in pan. Add onion and apple to drippings. Cook over medium heat for about 5 minutes, until slightly softened. Add cabbage, crumbled bacon, seasonings and water. Continue to cook over medium heat for a few minutes, stirring to make sure seasonings are mixed through the cabbage. Reduce heat to low. Cover and simmer for 20 to 30 minutes, stirring occasionally. If desired, stir in butter near the end of cooking time. Makes 6 to 8 servings.

You'll find lots of daffodil and tulip bulbs in garden centers. Plant them in late October or early November for springtime color...it's the ideal time!

Harvest
Sides & Salads

Baked German Potato Salad

Karen Wilson
Defiance, OH

This is my favorite recipe for German potato salad. It's perfect alongside grilled pork chops or brats on chilly fall days.

12 redskin potatoes
8 slices bacon
1-1/2 c. onions, chopped
3/4 c. brown sugar, packed
1/3 c. vinegar
1/3 c. sweet pickle juice

2/3 c. water, divided
2 t. dried parsley
1-1/2 t. celery seed
1 t. salt
4-1/2 t. all-purpose flour

In a large saucepan, cover potatoes with water. Cook over medium-high heat until fork-tender; drain. Cool; peel and slice potatoes into an ungreased 2-quart casserole dish. Set aside. In a skillet, cook bacon over medium heat until crisp. Drain bacon on paper towels, reserving 2 tablespoons drippings in skillet. Sauté onion in drippings until tender. Stir in brown sugar, vinegar, pickle juice, 1/3 cup water, parsley, celery seed and salt. Simmer, uncovered, for 5 to 10 minutes. Meanwhile, combine flour and remaining water in a cup; mix until smooth. Stir flour mixture into onion mixture. Bring to a full boil; cook and stir for 2 minutes. Pour over potatoes in dish; stir in crumbled bacon. Bake, uncovered, at 350 degrees for 30 minutes. Serve warm. Makes 8 servings.

Encourage table talk among dinner guests who don't know each other well. Just write each person's name on both sides of his or her placecard, where other guests can see it!

Welcome AUTUMN

Fruit-Stuffed Fall Acorn Squash

Edward Kielar
Whitehouse, OH

The fruity filling makes this acorn squash so colorful and tasty.

2 small acorn squash, halved
  and seeds removed
1/4 t. salt
2 c. tart apples, cored and
  chopped

3/4 c. fresh or frozen cranberries
1/4 c. brown sugar, packed
2 T. butter, melted
1/4 t. cinnamon
1/8 t. ground nutmeg

Place squash halves cut-side down in an ungreased 13"x9" baking pan.
Add one inch of hot water to pan. Bake, uncovered, at 350 degrees for
30 minutes. Drain water from pan; turn squash cut-side up. Sprinkle
with salt. Combine remaining ingredients in a bowl; spoon into squash
halves. Bake, uncovered, at 350 degrees for 40 to 50 minutes, until
squash is tender and filling is hot. Serves 4.

Squash Dressing

Donna Gay DeLoach
Summit, MS

*I like to cook sliced squash and onions in the summer when both are
fresh, and freeze it in quart containers to enjoy in fall or winter.*

2 c. yellow squash, sliced
1 sweet onion, sliced
salt and pepper to taste
2 c. cornbread, crumbled

2 eggs, beaten
1/2 c. butter, melted
10-3/4 oz. can cream of chicken
  soup

In a large saucepan, cover squash and onion with water. Cook over
medium heat until tender. Drain; season lightly with salt and generously
with pepper. Mix in cornbread, eggs, butter and chicken soup until well
blended. Spoon into a greased 13"x9" baking pan. Bake, uncovered,
at 350 degrees for 35 to 45 minutes, until bubbly and golden. Makes
10 to 12 servings.

Harvest
Sides & Salads

Cranberry-Broccoli Salad

Gerri Roth
Flushing, MI

*I love fresh broccoli and buy it all the time. I created
this salad to enjoy with fall meals.*

12-oz. pkg. broccoli slaw
1/2 c. dried cranberries
1/4 c. slivered almonds

1/3 c. raspberry vinaigrette
4 slices bacon, crisply cooked
   and crumbled

Combine broccoli slaw, cranberries and almonds in a bowl. Toss with
desired amount of vinaigrette; sprinkle with bacon. Cover and chill for
2 to 3 hours. Toss again before serving. Makes 6 servings.

Slow-Cooked Cinnamon Apples

Deborah Hamilton
Burlington, NC

*The scent of apples and cinnamon on an early fall day is wonderful!
Every fall when the fresh apples hit my local farmstand, this is the
first recipe I pull out. These apples are delicious over pork chops,
as a side dish or a dessert.*

6 baking apples, peeled, cored
   and sliced
1/2 c. light brown sugar, packed

2 t. cornstarch
1/2 t. cinnamon

Place apples in a 3-quart slow cooker; set aside. Combine remaining
ingredients in a small bowl; sprinkle over apples and toss gently. Cover
and cook on low heat setting for about 3 hours, until apples are tender.
Leftovers reheat well. Makes 4 servings.

For delicious apple desserts, some of
the best varieties are Granny Smith,
Gala, Jonagold and Honeycrisp.

Mexican Street Corn Salad

Stephanie Turner
Meridian, ID

This recipe reminds me of my old stomping grounds, San Diego.

5 ears sweet corn
1 pt. cherry or pear tomatoes,
    halved or quartered
1 avocado, pitted, peeled and
    cut into 1/2-inch cubes
1/2 c. red onion, finely diced

1/4 c. fresh cilantro, chopped
1/4 c. crumbled cotija or feta
    cheese
Optional: additional chopped
    fresh cilantro

Grill or steam corn just until tender; cool and slice kernels off cobs. Meanwhile, make Dressing; set aside. In a large bowl, combine corn, tomatoes, avocado, onion, cilantro and dressing. Gently stir to combine and coat evenly, being careful not to mash avocado. Top with crumbled cheese and additional cilantro, if desired. Serves 8.

Dressing:

1/2 c. mayonnaise
1 t. chili powder

1/2 t. garlic salt
zest and juice of 1 lime

Combine all ingredients; mix well.

For a clever porch display, carve your house number
into a pumpkin. Set it on the front steps and slip
a lighted votive inside.

Harvest
Sides & Salads

Bacon-Ranch Pasta Salad

Kimberly Brown
Burt, MI

We loved the flavor of a certain packaged bacon-ranch pasta salad mix. But, we wanted to have fresher veggies and fewer processed ingredients, so I decided to make it myself. Now I make this salad to take to family gatherings...I always leave with an empty bowl!

12-oz. pkg. mini bowtie
　pasta, uncooked
1 c. sour cream
1 c. mayonnaise
1-oz. pkg. ranch salad
　dressing mix

1/2 c. carrot, peeled and
　shredded
1/2 c. real bacon bits
1 c. frozen peas
1/2 c. shredded Cheddar cheese

Cook pasta according to package directions; drain and rinse with cold water to cool. Meanwhile, in a bowl, stir together sour cream, mayonnaise and dressing mix until well combined. In a large bowl, combine cooled pasta and carrot. Add sour cream mixture; mix well. Add bacon bits and peas; mix well. Stir in shredded cheese, a little at a time. Cover and chill for one hour, to allow flavors to combine. Makes 8 to 10 servings.

Enjoy autumn's harvest! Late-season farmers' markets are overflowing with squash and root vegetables that are tasty in stews and casseroles...apples, pears and blackberries are delicious in pies and preserves. Grab a basket and a friend and check it out!

Welcome AUTUMN

Cornbread Dressing with Bacon & Pecans

Lynnette Jones
East Flat Rock, NC

This delicious dressing has become a favorite of our family for the holidays.

4 slices applewood smoked
   bacon, chopped
1 c. onion, diced
1 c. celery, diced
6-1/2 c. cornbread, crumbled
1 t. ground sage

3/4 t. poultry seasoning
3/4 t. salt
1/2 t. pepper
6 T. butter, melted
1 c. chicken broth
1/2 c. chopped pecans, toasted

Add bacon to a Dutch oven over medium heat; cook until partially cooked but not crisp. Remove bacon to a paper towel, reserving drippings in pan. Add onion and celery to reserved drippings; sauté until tender and set aside. In a large bowl, combine crumbled bacon and cornbread; add seasonings. Stir in melted butter, chicken broth and onion mixture. Fold in pecans. Spoon mixture into a buttered 2-quart casserole dish; cover with aluminum foil. Bake at 375 degrees for 25 minutes. Remove foil and bake for another 10 minutes, or until top of dressing is a bit crusty. Serves 8.

Mix up a fresh poppy seed dressing for fruit salad. Combine 1/4 cup oil, 3 tablespoons honey, 2 tablespoons lemon juice and 1-1/2 teaspoons poppy seed. Drizzle over your favorite fruits... it's scrumptious with oranges, pineapple, apples and grapes.

Harvest
Sides & Salads

Baked Zucchini Fries

Jackie Smulski
Lyons, IL

A lightened-up version of deep-fried zucchini that I enjoy. When you have extra zucchini, this recipe will please everyone!

2 medium zucchini
1/4 c. all-purpose flour
2 eggs
3/4 c. Italian-seasoned dry
    bread crumbs
1/4 c. grated Parmesan cheese

1 T. fresh chives, minced
1/4 t. dried, minced onions
1 t. salt
1/4 t. pepper
Garnish: marinara sauce,
    warmed

Cut zucchini into 3-inch lengths, then into 1/2-inch thick spears. Place in a large bowl; sprinkle with flour. Toss to coat well and set aside. Beat eggs in a shallow dish. In another shallow dish, combine remaining ingredients except garnish. Dredge zucchini in eggs, then in crumb mixture. Arrange zucchini pieces without touching on a parchment paper-lined baking sheet. Bake at 400 degrees for 17 to 20 minutes, until zucchini is tender and beginning to turn golden. Serve with warm marinara sauce. Makes 4 to 6 servings.

Show your spirit...dress up a garden scarecrow in
a hometown football jersey!

Molly's Yams with Pineapple

Sheri Kohl
Wentzville, MO

This recipe has been enjoyed many times by everyone lucky enough to have known my friend Molly. I first tasted it at her house one Thanksgiving and was hooked! We enjoy it quite often in the fall and winter, and every time we eat it, we remember Molly and her wonderful hospitality. This recipe is delicious made with canned apricots, too.

30-oz. can cut yams, drained
1/4 c. brown sugar, packed
1/4 c. butter, melted
2 T. whipping cream
1 egg, beaten
1/2 t. salt
1/4 t. cinnamon
1/2 t. vanilla extract
1/4 c. plus 1 T. chopped walnuts,
 divided
8-oz. can pineapple tidbits,
 drained

Place yams in a large bowl; beat with an electric mixer on medium speed until smooth. Add brown sugar, butter, cream, egg, salt, cinnamon, vanilla and 1/4 cup walnuts. Beat well. Spread half of yam mixture in a buttered 8"x8" baking pan. Arrange pineapple tidbits on top. Add remaining yam mixture; garnish with remaining walnuts. Bake, uncovered, at 350 degrees for 20 minutes, or until heated through. Makes 4 to 6 servings.

Straw shopping totes from the thrift store make whimsical holders for autumn mums...just slip them over fence posts and fill with flowers.

Harvest
Sides & Salads

Cranberry Conserve

Betty Lou Wright
Fort Worth, TX

This scrumptious whole-fruit jam became part of my family's holiday meals about 20 years ago. It is my favorite dish to make at Thanksgiving and Christmas. Easy to prepare, makes the house smell heavenly and tastes so good on turkey & dressing, biscuits and toast. Serving it in a family heirloom glass bowl makes it even more special.

4 c. fresh cranberries
1 c. water
1 whole orange
1 c. raisins
2 to 2-1/2 c. sugar

1/2 c. finely chopped pecans
   or walnuts
3 1-pint glass or plastic
   containers with lids,
   sterilized

In a large saucepan, combine cranberries and water. Bring to a boil over medium-high heat. Reduce heat to medium; cover and simmer for about 8 minutes, until cranberry skins pop. Meanwhile, grate the zest from orange; peel, seed and dice the orange. Stir together cranberries, orange pieces and zest, raisins, sugar to taste and nuts. Cook over low heat, stirring often, for about 20 minutes, until mixture thickens. Remove from heat and cool. Chill several hours before serving. Spoon into containers; cover and keep refrigerated. Makes 3 pints.

Fresh cranberries can be kept frozen up to 12 months, so if you enjoy them, stock up every autumn when they're available and pop unopened bags in the freezer. You'll be able to add their fruity tang to recipes year 'round.

Welcome AUTUMN

Mom's Mexican Hominy

Sandy Coffey
Cincinnati, OH

A fun side to add to tacos for lunch or dinner.

1 lb. ground beef round
1 c. onion, chopped
1 clove garlic, minced
8-oz. pkg. shredded mild
   Cheddar cheese

15-1/2 oz. can hominy, drained
14-1/2 oz. can diced tomatoes
   with green chiles
10-3/4 oz. can tomato soup

Brown beef with onion and garlic in a skillet over medium heat; drain. Transfer mixture to a greased 2-quart casserole dish. Add remaining ingredients; stir well. Cover and bake at 350 degrees for 30 minutes, or until bubbly and cheese is melted. Serves 4 to 6.

Potato Chip Potatoes

Sharon Welch
LaCygne, TX

This is easy and good!

6 potatoes, peeled and cubed
1 c. potato chips, crushed
   and divided
1/4 to 1/2 c. dried, flaked onions

2 T. butter, melted
1 t. salt
1/4 t. pepper
Optional: sour cream

In a large bowl, combine potatoes, 1/2 cup potato chips, onions, melted butter, salt and pepper. Mix well; transfer to a greased 2-quart casserole dish. Sprinkle remaining potato chips on top. Bake, uncovered, at 350 degrees for 40 to 50 minutes, until potatoes are tender. Dollop with sour cream, if desired. Makes 6 servings.

Mini pumpkins make the sweetest placecards! Simply punch holes in paper tags, slip a ribbon though each and tie to the stem.

Harvest
Sides & Salads

Jalapeño Corn Casserole

Cindy Winfield
Nacogdoches, TX

An easy side dish your family will enjoy. This isn't spicy tasting, but chopped jalapeños could be added if desired.

6-oz. pkg. Mexican-style
   cornbread mix, divided
1 T. sugar
1 t. dried, flaked onions

salt and pepper to taste
14-3/4 oz. can cream-style corn
1 egg, beaten
1/4 c. butter, melted

Measure half of cornbread mix into a large bowl; reserve remaining mix for another recipe. Add remaining ingredients except butter; mix well. Pour batter into a greased 1-1/2 quart casserole dish; drizzle with melted butter. Bake at 350 degrees for 20 to 30 minutes. Cut into squares. Makes 4 to 6 servings.

If it's Thanksgiving now, Christmas can't be far away.
Double your favorite festive casseroles and side dishes,
and freeze half for Christmas dinner...what a time-saver!

Ila's Spinach Salad

Peggy Ann Hegelein
Binghamton, NY

This is a recipe from a very dear friend of mine. The dressing, hard-boiled eggs and crispy bacon can be prepared the night before, then just toss together the salad in a jiffy and serve.

3 eggs, hard-boiled, peeled and diced
6 slices bacon, crisply cooked and crumbled

8-oz. can sliced water chestnuts, drained
1 lb. fresh spinach, torn

Make Dressing; set aside. Combine all ingredients in a bowl; toss to mix and set aside. Pour Dressing over salad mixture; toss again and serve. Makes 4 servings.

Dressing:

1 c. oil
3/4 c. sugar
3/4 c. onion, chopped, or 2 T. dried, chopped onions

1/3 c. catsup
1/4 c. vinegar
1 T. Worcestershire sauce
1 t. salt

Combine all ingredients in a bowl or jar; whisk or shake well.

Jumping in leaf piles is a not-to-be-missed part of fall fun! No fallen leaves in your yard? Ask some neighbors with a big maple tree for permission to rake up their leaves...you'll have a ball!

Harvest
Sides & Salads

Coleslaw with a Kick

Karen Antonides
Gahanna, OH

*If you like horseradish, you will certainly enjoy this coleslaw.
It is easy to prepare and packs a little punch.*

1 c. mayonnaise-style salad
   dressing
2 T. prepared horseradish
2 t. white vinegar

2 T. sugar
salt to taste
16-oz. pkg. coleslaw mix

In a large bowl, mix together salad dressing, horseradish, vinegar and sugar; season with salt. Add coleslaw mix and stir to coat. Cover and refrigerate for 3 hours before serving, to allow flavors to blend. Makes 8 servings.

Marinated Cucumbers

Doreen Knapp
Stanfordville, NY

*I love cucumbers! I'm always looking to find different salads and
ways to use them...this one is simple and delicious.*

5 cucumbers, peeled and
   thinly sliced
1-1/4 c. red wine vinegar or
   cider vinegar
1 c. water

3 T. sugar
1 T. dried dill weed
2 cloves garlic, minced
1/4 t. salt
1/4 t. pepper

Place cucumber slices in a heat-proof glass bowl; set aside. In a saucepan over medium-high heat, combine remaining ingredients. Bring to a boil; reduce heat to medium-low. Simmer for 5 minutes, stirring occasionally, until sugar is dissolved. Pour marinade over cucumbers; toss to mix well. Cover and refrigerate for 24 hours before serving. Serves 6.

Mom's Amazing Baked Beans

Monique Chilelli
South Riding, VA

This dish has been in my family's recipe box since the early 1980s. It's great for serving up at family gatherings, potlucks and backyard barbecues. Everyone loves these baked beans and always comes back for second servings. We usually make two big trays of beans to take with us to our family & friends' get-togethers.

2 c. dried navy beans, rinsed and sorted
1 c. sweet onion, chopped
1 meaty smoked ham hock
1 t. salt
4 c. water

1/2 c. brown sugar, packed
1/4 c. catsup
1/4 c. dark molasses
1 t. dry mustard
1 t. baking soda

To a 4-quart slow cooker, add navy beans, onion, ham hock and salt; pour in water. Cover and cook on low setting up to 12 hours, checking occasionally, until water has been absorbed by beans. Remove ham hock and set aside to cool; drain most of remaining liquid. Shred ham from the hock and add to slow cooker along with remaining ingredients. Cover and continue cooking on low setting for 20 minutes, or until mixture thickens and flavors blend. Serves 6.

Decorate paper placemats with leaf prints...so easy, kids can do it. Brush leaves with a little poster paint and carefully lay in place. Cover with a paper towel and roll lightly with a rolling pin. Remove the towel, pull off the leaves...so pretty!

Harvest
Sides & Salads

Creamy Succotash with Bacon

Dale Duncan
Waterloo, IA

Succotash has always been a favorite on our Thanksgiving table. This recipe really takes it up a notch! It can be made up to two days ahead, too. Cook until beans and corn are tender; refrigerate along with cooked bacon. At serving time, reheat; stir in bacon and chives.

4 thick slices bacon, chopped
3/4 c. onion, chopped
10-oz. pkg. frozen baby
    lima beans
1/2 c. water

salt and pepper to taste
10-oz. pkg. frozen corn
1/2 c. whipping cream
1-1/2 t. fresh thyme, snipped
2 t. fresh chives, snipped

Cook bacon in a Dutch oven over medium heat until crisp. Drain bacon on paper towel, reserving 2 tablespoons drippings in pan. Add onion to skillet; sauté until tender. Add lima beans, water, salt and pepper; bring to a boil. Reduce heat to medium-low. Cover and simmer for 5 minutes, or until beans are partially cooked. Stir in corn, cream and thyme. Simmer another 5 minutes, or until vegetables are tender. Just before serving, stir in crumbled bacon and chives. Makes 6 servings.

As autumn evenings turn dark, light a candle or 2 at the family dinner table. It'll make an ordinary meal seem special!

Welcome AUTUMN

Grandma's Mac & Cheese

Tracy Meyers
Alexandria, KY

This recipe comes from my mother-in-law. My kids ask for her mac & cheese every holiday! We love it so much that she makes an extra batch so everyone has leftovers to take home. It's so good!

8-oz. pkg. rotini pasta, uncooked
8-oz. pkg. elbow macaroni, uncooked
3/4 c. butter, divided
8-oz. pkg. shredded Colby Jack cheese, divided
8-oz. pkg. shredded triple Cheddar-blend cheese, divided
4 slices American cheese, torn
1 c. milk
salt and pepper to taste

Cook pasta and macaroni according to package directions, just until tender. Drain; return to pan. Add 1/4 cup butter; stir until butter melts and coats pasta. Set pasta aside. In a large saucepan, melt remaining butter over low heat. Set aside 1/2 cup of each shredded cheese for topping. Add remaining cheeses and milk to melted butter; cook and stir until cheeses melt. Pour cheese mixture over pasta and stir well. Season with salt and pepper. Transfer to a buttered 3-quart casserole dish; top with reserved cheeses. Bake, uncovered, at 350 degrees for 45 to 60 minutes, until bubbly and golden. Makes 6 to 8 servings.

Add an extra can or 2 of soup, veggies or tuna to the grocery cart every week, then put aside these extras at home. Before you know it, you'll have a generous selection of canned goods for fall food drives.

Harvest
Sides & Salads

Slow-Cooker Red Cabbage with Apples

Carolyn Deckard
Bedford, IN

*In our family, we are great fans of red cabbage and apples.
This dish is a great go-with for pork chops.*

1 head red cabbage, coarsely
    shredded
2 tart red apples, cored and sliced
3 T. cider vinegar
3 T. water

2 T. sugar
1 T. butter, melted
1 t. salt
1/4 t. pepper

Combine all ingredients in a 4-quart slow cooker. Cover and cook on low setting for 6 to 8 hours, until cabbage is very tender. Stir again and serve. Makes 8 servings.

Jess's Broccoli Cornbread

Jess Brunink
Whitehall, MI

*My family loves this! It is really hearty and so good. Great as a side
with a roasted chicken...perfect for potlucks too. A yummy addition
is 5 slices of cooked and crumbled bacon.*

2 8-1/2 oz. pkgs. corn
    muffin mix
14-3/4 oz. can creamed corn
2/3 c. water

16-oz. pkg. frozen chopped
    broccoli, thawed
3/4 c. onion, diced

In a large bowl, mix all ingredients together. Pour into a greased 13"x9" baking pan. Bake, uncovered, at 350 degrees for one hour. Cool for 5 to 10 minutes; cut into squares. Makes 12 servings.

Small cheer and great welcome make a merry feast!
–William Shakespeare

Welcome AUTUMN

Oven-Roasted Potato Wedges

Patricia Nau
River Grove, IL

These potatoes are not like your usual oven-roasted potatoes.
The lemon juice gives it a flavor, all its own.

8 potatoes, quartered and
   cut into wedges
1 c. water
1/2 c. lemon juice
2 T. olive oil

2 t. garlic, chopped
2 t. kosher salt
1 t. lemon pepper
1 t. dried oregano

In a large bowl, toss together all ingredients. Spread mixture in a greased 13"x9" baking pan. Bake, uncovered, at 350 degrees for 2 hours, or until potatoes are fork-tender and most of the liquid is absorbed. Makes 4 to 6 servings.

Seasoned Baked Zucchini Rings

Julia Bondi
Chicago, IL

This is a recipe I made up because I like zucchini and my husband says it's boring! The salad seasoning really zaps it up. Serve with ranch dressing on the side.

3 T. olive oil
5 to 6 small zucchini, cut into
   rings, 1/4-inch thick
1 t. garlic powder

1/4 c. salad supreme seasoning,
   or to taste
pepper to taste

Spread oil on a baking sheet or shallow baking pan. Arrange zucchini rings in a single layer. Sprinkle evenly with seasonings. Bake at 350 degrees for 15 minutes, or until tender and lightly golden. Serve immediately. Makes 3 to 4 servings.

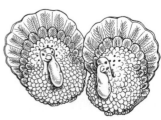

Vintage turkey salt & pepper shakers
brighten any autumn tabletop.

Harvest
Sides & Salads

Quinoa-Broccoli Balls

Martha Stapler
Sanford, FL

I was looking for a healthy version of a broccoli casserole. So I bought some quinoa and gave this a try...my hubby loved it!

2 c. cooked quinoa
1 c. broccoli, finely chopped
1/2 c. onion, finely chopped
1 c. shredded sharp
   Cheddar cheese

2 eggs, beaten
2 T. grated Parmesan cheese
1/2 t. garlic powder
1/2 t. salt
1/4 t. pepper

Combine all ingredients in a large bowl; mix well. With a small scoop, scoop mixture into balls on a parchment paper-lined rimmed baking sheet. Bake at 375 degrees for 20 to 25 minutes, until firm and lightly golden. Makes about 16 pieces.

Head out to a pick-your-own apple orchard for a day of fresh-air fun. The kids will love it, and you'll come home with bushels of the best-tasting apples for applesauce, cobblers and crisps!

Cauliflower-Broccoli Mixed Casserole

Sandy Coffey
Cincinnati, OH

A tasty dish combining my family members' favorite veggies.

1/2 head cauliflower, chopped
1/2 bunch broccoli, chopped
1/2 c. onion, sliced
10-3/4 oz. can cream of
   celery soup
1/4 c. evaporated milk

salt and pepper to taste
1-1/2 c. shredded Cheddar
   cheese
12 buttery round crackers,
   crushed
3 T. butter, sliced

Combine cauliflower, broccoli and onion in a large saucepan; cover with water. Cook over medium heat for 10 minutes, or until tender. Drain well. Spread mixture evenly in a greased 2-quart casserole dish; set aside. In another saucepan, combine celery soup, evaporated milk, salt and pepper; cook and stir until well blended. Spoon over vegetable mixture; sprinkle with cheese and crushed crackers. Dot with butter. Bake, uncovered, at 375 degrees for 20 minutes, or until heated through and cheese is melted. Makes 6 to 8 servings.

Set a packet of pumpkin seeds at each place setting for a fun, colorful favor...check end-of-season sales for bargains. Guests can save them to plant in next year's garden.

Harvest
Sides & Salads

Mom's Best Potato Salad

Wendy Jo Minotte
Duluth, MN

No one can make potato salad as good as Mom's! A plastic ice cream pail with a lid is a great way to transport this salad to your family gathering.

5 lbs. potatoes, peeled, cooked
    and diced
10 eggs, hard-boiled, peeled
    and diced

6 stalks celery, diced
1 c. onion, diced
salt and pepper to taste

In a roaster pan, combine potatoes, eggs, celery and onion; mix well. Add Sauce; mix thoroughly. Transfer to a large serving bowl with a tight-fitting lid; chill until ready to serve. Season with salt and pepper just before serving. Makes 10 to 12 servings.

Sauce:

2 c. mayonnaise-style salad
    dressing
1 c. milk

1 T. sugar
3/4 t. mustard

In a quart-size jar, combine all ingredients. Cover jar and shake until well blended, smooth and creamy.

The leaves fall, the wind blows, and the farm country slowly changes from the summer cottons into its winter wools.

– Henry Beston

Welcome AUTUMN

Tuscan Bread Salad

Irene Robinson
Cincinnati, OH

This is a delicious way to use fresh vegetables...
a great accompaniment for grilled steak.

3 c. Italian bread, sliced, toasted
   and cubed
2 c. arugula, torn into bite-size
   pieces

1 c. ripe tomato, chopped
1 c. cucumber, chopped
1/2 c. shredded Parmesan cheese
3/4 c. zesty Italian salad dressing

In a large salad bowl, combine bread cubes, arugula, tomato, cucumber and cheese. Toss to mix; drizzle with salad dressing and toss again. Makes 8 servings.

Cowboy Baked Beans

Jacki Smith
Fayetteville, NC

This slow-cooker recipe is hearty and perfect for large family gatherings. It's easy too! Put everything in the crock and it cooks all day. Serve with hamburgers, hot dogs and ribs.

1 lb. ground beef, browned
   and drained
2 16-oz. cans baked beans
16-oz. can pinto beans

15-1/2 oz. can navy beans
14-1/2 oz. can lima beans
18-oz. bottle barbecue sauce

Combine all ingredients in a 5-quart slow cooker, draining pinto, navy and lima beans. Stir well. Cover and cook on low setting for 6 to 8 hours. Makes 10 to 12 servings.

Bales of hay make comfy seating for a casual fall cookout.

Chilly-Day
Soups & Breads

Welcome AUTUMN

Turkey & Wild Rice Soup

Kathy Harris
Overland Park, KS

I love, love, love soup! This one is extra special and a great way to use that leftover turkey. This recipe was made up by my mother and me, one day after our Thanksgiving meal, since we already had all the ingredients on hand. Great to enjoy with some crusty bread while watching football in front of the television.

4 c. water
2 T. butter
1 t. salt, divided
1 c. wild rice, uncooked
4 slices bacon
2 c. onions, chopped
1-1/2 c. celery, chopped

2 cloves garlic, minced
6 c. turkey or chicken broth
3 c. roast turkey, chopped
1/4 t. pepper
1 c. whipping cream
2 T. fresh parsley, chopped

In a large saucepan over medium-high heat, combine water, butter and 1/2 teaspoon salt; bring to a boil. Stir in rice; return to a boil. Reduce heat to medium-low. Cover and simmer for 55 minutes, or until rice is tender. Drain, if necessary; set aside. Meanwhile, cook bacon in a large Dutch oven over medium heat until crisp. Drain bacon on paper towels, reserving drippings in Dutch oven. Sauté onions, celery and garlic in drippings until tender, being careful not to burn garlic. Stir in broth, turkey, remaining salt and pepper. Bring to a boil; reduce heat to medium-low. Cover and simmer for 5 minutes, or until heated through. Stir in cooked rice, crumbled bacon and cream. Simmer over medium heat for 15 minutes, or until slightly thickened. Stir in parsley and serve. Makes 8 servings.

Leftover turkey freezes well for up to 3 months. Cut into bite-size pieces, place in plastic freezer bags and pop in the freezer... ready to stir into hearty soups and casseroles whenever you are.

Chilly-Day
Soups & Breads

Onion-Cheese Bread

*Julie Perkins
Anderson, IN*

Whip up this warm bread to go with dinner tonight!

1-1/2 c. biscuit baking mix
1/2 c. onion, chopped
1 T. shortening
1 egg, lightly beaten

1/2 c. milk
1 c. shredded Cheddar cheese,
    divided
2 T. butter, melted

Add biscuit mix to a large bowl; set aside. In a skillet over medium heat, sauté onion in shortening until translucent. Meanwhile, in a small bowl, whisk together egg and milk. Add to biscuit mix; stir until moistened. Stir in onion and 1/2 cup cheese. Spread batter in a greased 8"x8" baking pan. Top with remaining cheese; drizzle with butter. Bake at 400 degrees for 20 to 25 minutes. Cut into squares. Makes 9 servings.

Greek Lemon-Chicken Soup

*Pat Martin
Riverside, CA*

A culinary trip to Greece without leaving home! This soup called Avgolemono is served at our local Greek restaurant and I've adapted the recipe for our family. It is comfort and flavor at its best!

8 c. chicken broth
1/2 to 3/4 c. orzo pasta,
    uncooked
3 eggs, beaten

juice of 2 lemons
1 to 2 c. cooked chicken, diced
    or shredded
salt and pepper to taste

In a soup pot, bring chicken broth to a boil over high heat. Add orzo; cook for 6 to 7 minutes. Do not drain; reduce heat to a simmer. Meanwhile, beat together eggs and lemon juice in a small bowl. When orzo is cooked, gradually add one cup of hot broth to egg mixture, whisking constantly. Add egg mixture and chicken to hot broth; gently heat through, but do not boil. Season with salt and pepper. Serves 6 to 8.

If the soup tastes a little bland, it may just need
a little more salt to perk up the flavors. Give it a try!

Cheesy Vegetable Soup

Tiffany Jones
Batesville, AR

*One day I was hungry for some soup and came up with
this yummy recipe. So hearty...I hope you like it too!*

14-1/2 oz. can Italian-seasoned
    diced tomatoes
14-1/2 oz. can Italian stewed
    tomatoes
14-1/2 oz. can diced tomatoes
    with green chiles
15-oz. can corn, drained
14-1/2 oz. can cut carrots,
    drained
14-1/2 oz. can cut green
    beans, drained

32-oz. container vegetable broth
1 t. dried basil
1 t. garlic powder
1 t. onion powder
salt and pepper to taste
16-oz. pkg. rotini pasta,
    uncooked
8-oz. pkg. pasteurized process
    cheese, cubed
8-oz. container sour cream

In a large soup pot, combine all tomatoes with juice, corn, carrots, green
beans, vegetable broth and seasonings. Bring to a boil over high heat;
stir in pasta. Reduce heat to medium; stir in cheese and sour cream.
Cook until pasta is tender, about 10 minutes. Makes 6 to 8 servings.

Set out a country-style welcome at the front door. Arrange
fallen autumn leaves on a plain jute doormat and spray carefully
with indoor-outdoor paint in russet, brown or gold.
Remove leaves after paint has dried...how clever!

Chilly-Day
Soups & Breads

Slow-Cooker Taco Soup

Tyson Trecannelli
Falling Waters, WV

I usually have to double this recipe...everyone comes back for more!
I serve this with corn muffins. Add a sprinkle of shredded Cheddar
cheese, a dollop of sour cream and/or guacamole and get rave reviews!

1 lb. ground beef
3/4 c. onion, diced
28-oz. diced tomatoes
15-1/2 oz. can Great
   Northern beans
15-1/2 oz. can chili beans

14-3/4 oz. can cream-style corn
8-oz. can tomato sauce
1/2 c. water
1-1/4 oz. pkg. taco
   seasoning mix

Brown beef with onion in a skillet over medium heat. Drain; transfer
to a 4-quart slow cooker. Stir in remaining ingredients, including liquid
from tomatoes, beans and corn. Cover and cook on low setting for 7 to
8 hours. Makes 6 to 8 servings.

Cornmeal Muffins

Bev Traxler
British Columbia, Canada

Great for breakfast, alongside soup or even for snacking! Be creative
and add some shredded Cheddar cheese, diced onion or jalapeños,
or even some crispy bacon.

1 c. cornmeal
1 c. all-purpose flour
2 T. sugar
4 t. baking powder

1/2 t. salt
1 egg, beaten
1 c. milk
2 T. shortening, melted

In a bowl, mix together cornmeal, flour, sugar, baking powder and
salt; set aside. In another bowl, whisk together egg, milk and melted
shortening. Add to cornmeal mixture; stir until moistened. Spoon batter
into paper-lined muffin cups, filling 2/3 full. Bake at 400 degrees for
25 minutes. Makes about one dozen.

Jelly Corn Muffins variation: Fill muffin cups 1/4 full; add a teaspoon
of jelly to each. Cover with more batter and bake as directed.

Italian Sausage & Vegetable Soup

Jo Ann
Gooseberry Patch

A great make-ahead soup recipe! It becomes even more
flavorful when you reheat it the next day.

1/2 lb. ground Italian pork
   sausage
1 onion, finely chopped
1 clove garlic, minced
3 14-oz. cans chicken broth
1/2 c. white wine or
   chicken broth
28-oz. can crushed tomatoes in
   tomato purée
2 zucchini, quartered lengthwise
   and sliced

2 carrots, peeled and diced
3 stalks celery, diced
1 green pepper, diced
1 t. dried basil
1/2 t. dried oregano
1/2 c. orzo pasta, uncooked
1/2 t. salt
1/2 t. pepper
Optional: 2/3 c. shredded
   Parmesan cheese

Brown sausage in a Dutch oven over medium heat. Drain, reserving a
small amount of drippings in pan. Add onion and garlic; cook just until
tender. Add chicken broth, wine or broth, tomatoes in purée, vegetables
and seasonings; bring to a boil over high heat. Stir in pasta. Reduce
heat to medium and simmer for 15 to 20 minutes, until vegetables and
pasta are tender. Season with salt and pepper. Top servings with
Parmesan cheese, if desired. Makes 8 servings.

Gourds and mini pumpkins left from Halloween can be
put to charming new use at Thanksgiving. Simply spray them
gold with craft paint to tuck into harvest centerpieces.

Chilly-Day
Soups & Breads

Butter Bean Soup

Krista Marshall
Fort Wayne, IN

This was one of the first recipes I learned to make as a newlywed,
20 years ago. I love that it uses canned beans, so it's budget-friendly.
You can add whatever veggies you have on hand in the fridge too.
Since it takes less than an hour, it's great for busy fall and
winter weeknights.

3 T. oil
1/2 c. onion, chopped
3 stalks celery, chopped
2 carrots, peeled and chopped
1 to 2 zucchini, chopped
salt and pepper to taste
2 cloves garlic, minced

3 T. all-purpose flour
2 32-oz. containers
   chicken broth
2 15-1/2 oz. cans baby butter
   beans, drained
1 t. dried basil

Heat oil in a large soup pot over medium heat. Add onion, celery, carrots
and zucchini; season with salt and pepper. Cook until soft, about 5 to
7 minutes, stirring often. Add garlic; cook for one more minute. Sprinkle
vegetables with flour; cook and stir for one minute. Gradually add
chicken broth, stirring until smooth. Add butter beans and basil; bring
to a boil. Reduce heat to medium-low. Simmer for 20 to 25 minutes,
stirring occasionally, until slightly thickened. Makes 6 to 8 servings.

Serve a variety of cheeses with a soup supper...perfect for guests
to nibble on! Arrange brightly colored autumn leaves on a clear
glass plate, then top with another glass plate to hold them in place.
Fill with assorted cheeses, crackers and crisp apple slices.

Autumn Day Chili

Angela Bissette
Wilson, NC

When autumn arrived, my mother always had a pot of her delicious chili cooking. I created this simple, yet tasty recipe in honor of her and my favorite season. For a spicier chili, use hot salsa, or replace the 28-ounce can of diced tomatoes with a 14-1/2 ounce can of diced tomatoes plus one 10-ounce can of diced tomatoes with green chiles.

2 lbs. ground beef or turkey
28-oz. can diced tomatoes
16-oz. jar salsa
2 15-1/2 oz. cans light red
    kidney beans, drained

2 15-1/2 oz. cans dark red
    kidney beans, drained
1 onion, diced
1 green pepper, diced

Brown beef or turkey in a stockpot over medium heat; drain. Stir in undrained tomatoes and remaining ingredients; bring to a boil. Reduce heat to low and simmer for 2 hours, stirring occasionally. Makes 8 servings.

Freeze chili in small containers...later, pop in the microwave for chili dogs, nachos or baked potatoes at a moment's notice.
A terrific time–saver among all the fall activities!

Chilly-Day
Soups & Breads

Fiesta Popcorn Cornbread

Jackie Smulski
Lyons, IL

*This cornbread is fun to make and fun to eat! It goes well
with fried chicken or barbecued ribs.*

4 c. popped popcorn
1 c. yellow cornmeal
2 T. sugar
2 t. baking powder
1/2 t. salt
1 egg, beaten
1 c. milk

1/4 c. oil
1 c. shredded Cheddar
    Jack cheese
4-oz. can diced mild green
    chiles, drained
2-oz. jar diced pimentos, drained

Check popcorn for any unpopped kernels. In a blender, process popcorn
until finely ground; transfer to a large bowl. Add cornmeal, sugar,
baking powder and salt; stir well and set aside. In a small bowl, beat
together egg, milk and oil; stir into popcorn mixture just until blended.
Scatter cheese, chiles and pimentos over batter; stir until evenly
distributed. Pour batter into a greased 8"x8" baking pan. Bake at
400 degrees for 25 minutes, or until lightly golden at the edges. Cut
into squares. Makes 9 servings.

For placecards that are oh-so-sweet, have the kids trace around
their hands on construction paper, then color with crayons
to create turkeys. Grandma will love it!

Double Pig Potato Soup

Beckie Apple
Grannis, AR

My twist on an old family favorite. This potato soup is so thick and rich...my husband says all you need to make a complete meal is a bowl, a spoon and a big appetite! Serve with crackers or cornbread and enjoy.

14-1/2 oz. can chicken broth
4 c. hot water
4 russet potatoes, peeled and
    cut in 1/2-inch cubes
1 c. onion, coarsely chopped
2 stalks celery, thinly sliced
2 carrots, peeled and thinly sliced
1-1/2 c. milk
5-oz. can cooked ham, diced

1/2 c. real bacon bits
4 slices American cheese,
    chopped
1/2 t. garlic powder
1/2 t. salt
1/4 t. pepper
1/2 c. instant mashed
    potato flakes

In a large stockpot, combine chicken broth and water; bring to a low boil over medium heat. Add potatoes, onion, celery and carrots; cook until vegetables are just tender. Stir in remaining ingredients except potato flakes; cook and stir until cheese melts. Add potato flakes; stir until blended. Remove from heat; soup will thicken on standing. Makes 6 servings.

Whip up some cozy throws in bright red or russet plaid fleece... snip fringe all around the edges. Perfect for tailgating, or for snuggling on a chilly night! They're so easy, you can make one for each member of the family in no time at all.

Chilly-Day
Soups & Breads

Cream of Sweet Corn & Ham Chowder

Bethi Hendrickson
Danville, PA

This creamy soup is quick to fix and so good! A great way to use that leftover holiday ham.

1 russet potato, peeled and diced
2 10-3/4 oz. cans cream of
   sweet corn soup
15-1/4 oz. can corn, drained
1 c. cooked ham, shredded
1 c. milk

1 c. regular or fat-free
   half-and-half
1 T. ham soup base
Garnish: 1/2 c. shredded
   Cheddar cheese

In a saucepan, cover potato with water. Cook over medium-high heat until fork-tender; drain. Meanwhile, in a stockpot or Dutch oven, combine remaining ingredients except garnish; mix well. Cook over low heat until heated through. Add cooked potato and heat through, about 5 minutes. Serve in soup bowls, topped with a few pinches of cheese. Makes 8 servings.

Bacon, Cheese & Potato Chowder

Gladys Kielar
Whitehouse, OH

This hearty chowder is ready in just 20 minutes and it's so delicious. Save a couple slices of bacon from breakfast for it!

3 c. fat-free milk
10-3/4 oz. can cream of
   potato soup
2 c. frozen diced southern-style
   hashbrowns

1 c. sharp Cheddar cheese
2 slices bacon, crisply cooked
   and crumbled
1/4 c. green onions, thinly sliced

Combine milk and potato soup in a large saucepan; stir in hashbrowns. Bring to a boil over high heat, stirring occasionally. Reduce heat to medium-low. Simmer for 10 minutes, stirring often. Ladle into bowls; top with cheese, bacon and onions. Serves 2 to 4.

Slow-Cooker Smoked Sausage Chili

Darcy Geiger
Columbia City, IN

*This soup is really delicious! It is one of my daughter's favorites...
she requests it all of the time. This recipe makes enough to serve
a crowd, or freeze any leftovers for another meal.*

2 15-1/2 oz. cans cannellini
  beans, drained and rinsed
2 15-1/2 oz. cans garbanzo
  beans, drained and rinsed
2 15-1/2 oz. cans Great Northern
  beans, drained and rinsed
6-oz. pkg. long grain & wild
  rice, uncooked
2 32-oz. containers
  chicken broth

2 4-oz. cans diced green chiles
2 13-1/2 oz. pkgs. smoked
  turkey sausage, cut into
  bite-size pieces
1 to 2 c. frozen corn
1 onion, diced
1-1/2 t. ground cumin
1-1/2 t. salt
1-1/2 t. pepper

Add all ingredients to a 6-quart slow cooker; stir together. Cover and
cook on low setting for 6 to 8 hours. Makes 10 to 12 servings.

Garnish bowls of chili with a dollop of chipotle cream...tasty!
Combine 1/2 cup sour cream and one teaspoon diced canned
chipotle peppers in adobo sauce. Season with salt and pepper
to taste and spoon onto chili.

Chilly-Day
Soups & Breads

Bacon Biscuit Wedges

Kathy Grashoff
Fort Wayne, IN

*This tasty warm bread is like a savory scone. Serve it
with butter alongside your favorite soup, or even topped
with sausage gravy for breakfast.*

2 c. all-purpose flour
4 slices bacon, crisply cooked
   and crumbled
2 t. baking powder

1/2 t. salt
1/4 c. shortening
2/3 to 1 c. milk
1 T. butter, melted

In a bowl, combine flour, bacon, baking powder and salt. With a fork,
cut in shortening until mixture resembles coarse crumbs. Stir in enough
milk to form a soft, moist dough. On a floured surface, gently knead
dough 5 to 6 times, until no longer sticky. Shape dough into a ball.
Place on a greased baking sheet; flatten into an 8-inch circle. With a
sharp knife, score top into 8 wedges. Bake at 400 degrees for 15 to
21 minutes, until risen and lightly golden. Brush with melted butter;
cut apart wedges. Serve warm. Serves 8.

Yummy Cheese Biscuits

Judy Taylor
Butler, MO

*A friend shared this yummy recipe with me. Add as much onion
as you want, and a dash of garlic powder...it gives a great flavor!*

7-1/2 oz. tube refrigerated
   biscuits
1 c. mayonnaise

8-oz. pkg. finely shredded
   Parmesan cheese
1/2 c. onion, finely chopped

Bake biscuits according to package directions; cool. Split biscuits and
return to baking sheet; set aside. Combine remaining ingredients in
a bowl; mix well. Spoon evenly onto biscuit halves. Place under hot
broiler until golden and cheese is melted. Watch very closely, as they
can burn fast. Serve hot. Makes 14 biscuits.

Wrap glass votives with autumn leaves, secured with
strands of raffia. So pretty!

Pumpkin Soup with Cheese Toasts

Wendy Meadows
Spring Hill, FL

Several years ago, I had a small pumpkin patch. After donating most of my pumpkins to the school art club, I had a few left over. I wanted to come up with a way to use the remaining pumpkins, aside from carving and making pies. I was pleased with the result!

1 T. butter
3-1/2 c. fresh pumpkin, peeled
   and cubed
3/4 c. carrots, peeled
   and chopped

1/2 c. sweet onion, chopped
2-1/2 c. lower-sodium
   chicken broth
1/4 c. half-and-half
1/8 t. salt

Melt butter in a large saucepan over medium-high heat. Add pumpkin, carrot and onion; sauté for 12 minutes. Add chicken broth; bring to a boil. Reduce heat to medium-low; cover and simmer for 30 minutes. Remove from heat; stir in half-and-half and salt. Transfer hot mixture to a blender. Add lid, removing center piece in lid to allow steam to escape. Cover opening with a folded towel to avoid spattering; process until smooth. Return to pan and heat through, as desired. Serve with Cheese Toasts. Serves 4.

Cheese Toasts:

4 slices French bread   3/4 c. shredded Swiss cheese

Arrange bread slices on a baking sheet. Place under broiler for one minute, or until lightly toasted. Turn slices over; top evenly with cheese. Broil for one minute, or until cheese is bubbly.

I would rather sit on a pumpkin and have it all
to myself, than be crowded on a velvet cushion.
–Henry David Thoreau

Chilly-Day
Soups & Breads

Flo's Cream of Vegetable Soup

Michelle Geraghty
Whitman, MA

A dear friend shared this recipe with me many years ago, and it has remained a favorite with my family. I've also used frozen broccoli to make cream of broccoli soup. Any frozen vegetable will do!

1/2 to 1 c. onion, finely chopped
1/4 c. plus 2 t. butter, divided
2 16-oz. pkgs. frozen
   mixed vegetables
3 c. boiling water

3 envs. chicken bouillon powder
2 T. all-purpose flour
1 c. low-fat milk
1/3 c. light cream
pepper to taste

In a large skillet over medium heat, sauté onion in 2 teaspoons butter until tender. Add frozen vegetables and sauté for 5 minutes. Add boiling water and bouillon; simmer over low heat for 30 minutes. Meanwhile, melt remaining butter in a large stockpot over medium heat; add flour. Cook and stir for 3 to 5 minutes, until mixture is deep golden. Slowly pour in milk and cream; stir well. Add vegetable mixture and mix well. Season with pepper; heat through over low heat. Serves 6 to 8.

The holidays are just around the corner...time to check your spice rack! Crush a pinch of each spice. If it has a fresh, zingy scent, it's still good. Toss out old-smelling spices and stock up on any that you've used up during the year.

Day-After-Thanksgiving Turkey Soup

Jennie Gist
Gooseberry Patch

My dad loved his turkey soup, every year after our Thanksgiving dinner. He wasn't choosy...he enjoyed it any way I made it! This is a favorite. If you like, add some diced potatoes along with the other vegetables, or stir in some soup pasta once the broth comes to a boil.

2 T. butter	1 T. tomato paste
2 yellow onions, diced	6 c. turkey or chicken broth
3 carrots, peeled and thinly sliced	3 c. cooked turkey, diced
3 stalks celery, thinly sliced	1/2 t. dried thyme
3 cloves garlic, minced	salt and pepper to taste

Melt butter in a Dutch oven over medium heat; add onions, carrots, celery and garlic. Cook, stirring occasionally, for about 5 minutes, until vegetables are soft. Stir in tomato paste and cook for one more minute. Stir in broth, turkey and thyme. Bring to a boil; reduce heat to medium-low. Cover and simmer for 30 minutes. Season with salt and pepper. Serves 4 to 6.

Thanksgiving is so family-centered...why not have a post-holiday potluck with friends, the weekend after Turkey Day? Everyone can bring their favorite "leftovers" concoctions and relax together.

Chilly-Day
Soups & Breads

Potato Rosemary Rolls

Linda Murray
Brentwood, NH

This is my granddaughter's favorite roll recipe that she requests at the holidays. I generally use the bread maker for mixing, but have also done it the old-fashioned way by hand.

1 c. plus 2 T. very warm water,
   110 to 115 degrees
2 T. olive oil
2 T. non-fat dry milk
1/2 c. instant mashed
   potato flakes
1 T. sugar
1 t. dried rosemary

1 t. salt
3 c. bread flour
1-1/2 t. bread machine yeast
1 T. cornmeal
1 egg, beaten, or 2 t. butter,
   melted
2 t. kosher salt

To a bread machine, add warm water, olive oil, dry milk, potato flakes, sugar, rosemary, salt, bread flour and yeast in order directed by manufacturer. Select Dough cycle and press start. *Divide dough into 12 pieces. Roll each into a 10-inch rope; coil rope and tuck in the end so that it comes up through the center, tying in a knot. Place rolls on a cornmeal-dusted baking sheet, 2 inches apart. Cover and let rise for 45 minutes. Brush tops with beaten egg or melted butter; lightly sprinkle with salt. Bake at 375 degrees for 15 to 20 minutes, until golden. Makes one dozen.

To mix dough by hand: Combine listed ingredients in a large bowl; beat with an electric mixer on medium speed until blended. Turn dough into a greased bowl; cover with a tea towel and let rise until double in bulk. Follow directions, starting at * above.

Herb butter is delicious on fresh-baked breads. Simply blend chopped fresh herbs into softened butter and spoon into a crock. Choose from parsley, dill, tarragon and chives, or create your own special herb garden mixture.

Ginger Pork Meatball & Noodle Soup

*Marian Buckley
Fontana, CA*

My family enjoys this soup as a change of pace. The meatballs can be made ahead and refrigerated until you're ready to make the soup.

1 lb. ground pork
1/4 c. panko bread crumbs
1 egg, beaten
1 T. water
3 cloves garlic, minced
1 T. fresh ginger, peeled
   and grated
1/2 t. red pepper flakes

salt and pepper to taste
12 c. low-sodium chicken broth
1/4 c. low-sodium soy sauce
1 t. rice vinegar
12-oz. pkg. narrow egg noodles,
   uncooked
4 c. baby spinach
Garnish: sliced green onions

In a large bowl, combine pork, panko crumbs, egg, water, garlic, ginger, red pepper flakes, salt and pepper. Mix well, using your hands; shape into small meatballs. Place meatballs on a plate; cover and chill for 20 minutes. Meanwhile, in a large pot over high heat, combine chicken broth, soy sauce and vinegar; bring to a boil. Add meatballs and noodles. Reduce heat to medium-low. Simmer for about 15 minutes, until noodles are tender and meatballs are cooked through. Add spinach; cook and stir until wilted. Ladle soup into bowls; garnish with onions. Serves 6.

Come, ye thankful people, come,
Raise the song of harvest home!
–Henry Alford

Chilly-Day
Soups & Breads

Leek & Potato Soup

Delores Lakes
Mansfield, OH

*When there is a nip in the air, hot soup is something I look
forward to. This delicious, easy and good-for-you soup
will be one of your favorites, too.*

3 T. butter
3 leeks, white parts only,
   thinly sliced
3/4 c. onion, thinly sliced
3 potatoes, peeled and
   thinly sliced

3 c. chicken broth
salt and white pepper to taste
1-1/2 c. milk
1/4 c. whipping cream or half-
   and-half

Melt butter in a large saucepan over medium heat. Add leeks and onion;
cook until partially softened. Add potatoes; stir in chicken broth and
cook over low heat for 30 minutes, or until vegetables are all very soft.
Purée mixture in a blender or use an immersion blender; season with
salt and pepper. Return purée to saucepan and bring to a gentle boil
over low heat, stirring constantly. Add milk and cream; heat through,
but do not boil. Makes 6 servings.

Keep a variety of thermoses on hand and fill each with
a different warming soup. So easy to tote along and share
during a chilly fall game, or tag with soup names and
set out on a party table.

Creamy Chicken Noodle Soup

Hollie Moots
Marysville, OH

*Nothing says comfort like chicken noodle soup! My boys were
enthusiastic taste-testers as I worked to perfect this recipe.
We love to eat it in big crocks with warm homemade bread...yum!*

1 T. butter
1/2 c. onion, chopped
1 stalk celery, chopped
1 carrot, peeled and sliced
1/2 t. dried parsley
8 c. water

8 t. chicken bouillon granules
6 c. wide egg noodles, uncooked
2 10-3/4 oz. cans cream of
   chicken soup
3 c. cooked chicken, cubed
1 c. sour cream

Melt butter in a skillet over medium heat. Add onion, celery, carrot
and parsley; sauté until tender. Meanwhile, bring water to a boil in a
large soup pot. Add bouillon and stir to dissolve; add noodles. Cook,
uncovered, for 10 to 12 minutes, until noodles are tender. Do not drain.
Add chicken soup, chicken and vegetable mixture; heat through.
Remove from heat; stir in sour cream and serve. Makes 6 servings.

Longing for Mom's old-fashioned homemade egg noodles? Try
frozen egg noodles from your grocer's frozen food section.
Thicker and heartier than dried noodles, these homestyle
noodles cook up quickly in all your favorite recipes.

Chilly-Day
Soups & Breads

Peanut Butter Bread

Judy Lange
Imperial, PA

The kids will run to the kitchen for this after-school snack after getting off the bus. You'd better make a few loaves!

2 c. all-purpose flour
1/3 c. sugar
2 t. baking powder
1 t. salt

1 egg, beaten
1 c. milk
3/4 c. creamy peanut butter
Garnish: favorite jelly

In a large bowl, combine flour, sugar, baking powder and salt. Add egg, milk and peanut butter; stir until combined. Pour batter into a greased 8"x4" loaf pan. Bake at 350 degrees for 50 minutes, or until a toothpick inserted in center comes out clean. Turn out of pan; slice and serve with jelly. Makes one loaf.

Quick Quesadilla

Anna McMaster
Portland, OR

Sometimes my son wants just a little more for lunch with his bowl of soup. This is ready in no time at all, and he loves it!

6-inch flour tortilla
1 slice favorite cheese

1 T. red pepper, chopped
1 t. green onion, sliced

Place tortilla on a microwave-safe plate. Top with cheese slice, pepper and onion; fold in half. Microwave on high setting for 15 to 20 seconds, until cheese begins to melt. Cut into wedges and serve. Makes one serving.

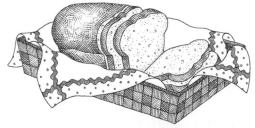

Quick breads taste best when wrapped and stored overnight at room temperature. They'll slice more easily too.

Welcome AUTUMN

South-of-the-Border Soup

Barbara Imler
Noblesville, IN

One day I was wondering what to do with some leftover pork roast, and I came up with this recipe. It's super easy...almost everything is from the pantry and it can be on the table in minutes. My husband doesn't usually care for "south of the border" flavors, but asks me to make this soup often. He loves it!

1 T. butter or oil
3/4 c. onion, chopped
1/2 green pepper, chopped
2 cloves garlic, minced
14-1/2 oz. can diced fire-roasted
   tomatoes
4-oz. chopped green chiles
32-oz. container chicken broth
14-oz. can beef broth

2 15-1/2 oz. cans hominy,
   drained
2 c. roast pork, cut into
   1/2-inch cubes
3/4 t. dried oregano
1/2 t. ground cumin
1/4 t. pepper
Optional: 1 t. salt
Garnish: hot pepper sauce

Heat butter or oil in a large soup pot over medium heat. Add onion, green pepper and garlic; sauté until onion is translucent and pepper is soft. Add undrained tomatoes and chiles. Stir in remaining ingredients except salt and garnish; simmer for 10 minutes. Add a little water, if additional liquid is needed. Season with salt, if needed. Serve with hot sauce. Makes 4 to 6 servings.

Start a delicious soup supper tradition on Halloween night.
Soup stays simmering hot while you hand out treats, and it isn't
too filling, so everyone has more room to nibble on goodies!

Chilly-Day
Soups & Breads

Slow-Cooker Lentil & Rice Soup

Doreen Knapp
Stanfordville, NY

This was my favorite soup that my mom used to make. Now I make it, and it's become my oldest son's favorite soup. It's bittersweet whenever I make it...Mom would have loved my two boys. It's a hearty soup that has such great flavor from the smoked pork hocks.

16-oz. pkg. brown lentils,
    rinsed and sorted
3 stalks celery, diced
3 carrots, peeled and diced
1 yellow onion, diced
2 cubes chicken bouillon cubes
1 lb. smoked pork hocks
4 to 8 c. water
2 c. cooked rice
Garnish: grated Parmesan cheese

In a 5-quart slow cooker, combine lentils, celery, carrots, onion, bouillon cubes and pork hocks. Add enough water to fill crock 3/4 full, making sure hocks are covered. Cover and cook on high setting for 2 to 4 hours. Check lentils occasionally for doneness; add more water, if needed. When soup is done, remove hocks to a plate; let cool. Cut off meat and return to soup. To serve, divide cooked rice among soup bowls; ladle soup over rice. Top with Parmesan cheese. Makes 4 servings.

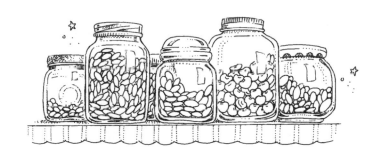

Watch for old-fashioned clear glass canisters at tag sales
and flea markets...perfect countertop storage for
dried beans and pasta.

Slow-Cooker Chicken Chili

Mary Jefferson Rabon
Mobile, AL

A game-day favorite! This has become known as our National Championship Soup. We have made it for the many championship games our Alabama Crimson Tide has played in....and won!

2 boneless, skinless chicken
   breasts
14-1/2 oz. can diced tomatoes
   with green chiles
15-1/4 oz. can corn
15-1/2 oz. can black beans,
   drained and rinsed
1-oz. pkg. ranch salad
   dressing mix

1 T. chili powder
1 t. ground cumin
1 t. onion powder
8-oz. pkg. light cream cheese,
   softened
Garnish: shredded Cheddar
   cheese
tortilla chips

Place chicken in a 5-quart slow cooker. Add tomatoes with juice, corn with juice and beans. Top with salad dressing mix and seasonings; stir together. Place cream cheese on top. Cover and cook on low setting for 6 to 8 hours. Stir cream cheese into chili. Use 2 forks to shred chicken in slow cooker; stir together. Serve soup topped with Cheddar cheese, with tortilla chips on the side. Makes 10 servings.

Serve savory stews in edible mini pumpkins, just for fun! Cut tops off pumpkins, scoop out seeds and brush lightly with oil. Bake on a baking sheet at 350 degrees for 30 to 40 minutes, until tender. Ladle in hot stew...yum!

Chilly-Day
Soups & Breads

Cowboy Cornbread

Tina Goodpasture
Meadowview, VA

I manage a grist mill that was built in the 1790s. We grind our cornmeal with stones, and it makes the best cornmeal. We don't use any preservatives. We also sell jams, jellies and butter that are made by the local Amish. This cornbread is the best ever...served warm with Amish butter and jam, it's better than dessert!

2 c. biscuit baking mix
1 c. yellow cornmeal
3/4 c. sugar
1/2 t. baking soda
1/2 t. salt

2 eggs, beaten
1 c. butter, melted
1 c. half-and-half, whole milk
  or buttermilk

Combine all ingredients in a large bowl; mix just until moistened. Spread batter in a greased cast-iron skillet or 13"x9" baking pan. Bake at 350 degrees for 25 to 30 minutes, until golden on top. Cut into wedges or squares. Makes 12 servings.

If you love cornbread with a crisp golden crust, bake it
in a cast-iron skillet, greased and preheated
before adding the batter.

Spicy Chicken Curry Veggie Soup *Julie Dossantos*
Fort Pierce, FL

This recipe came about one day when I realized I was out of cumin while planning to make white chicken chili. So I added curry powder instead...it turned out fantastic! A dollop of sour cream would be a wonderful garnish.

2 boneless, skinless chicken
   breasts
1 t. olive oil
1/2 onion, chopped
1 c. baby carrots, chopped
2 stalks celery, chopped
3/4 c. frozen corn
1 t. garlic, diced
15-1/2 oz. can white beans,
   drained
4-oz. can diced green chiles
1 t. curry powder
1 t. chili powder
1 t. dried oregano
1/4 t. cayenne pepper
salt and pepper to taste
32-oz. container chicken broth
1/2 c. whole milk or whipping
   cream
tortilla chips

Grill or cook chicken breasts as desired; chop and set aside. In a large soup pot, heat oil over medium heat. Add onion, carrots and celery; cook for 5 to 7 minutes, until onion is tender. Add corn and garlic; cook for 4 to 5 minutes. Add beans, chiles and seasonings; cook for 4 to 5 minutes. Stir in chicken broth; cover and bring to a simmer. Reduce heat to low; simmer for 10 to 15 minutes. Stir in chicken and milk or cream. Simmer for another 5 minutes, stirring occasionally; do not boil. Serve with tortilla chips. Makes 4 to 6 servings.

Collect autumn leaves to use as coasters for a burst of color on the dinner table. Write guests' names along the edge with a gold or copper paint pen...they'll double as placecards too.

Chilly-Day
Soups & Breads

Chicken & Wild Rice Soup

Valerie Bryant
Riverview, FL

We were stationed at Loring Air Force Base in Maine. When I had surgery, one of the ladies from the base chapel kindly brought this soup to us. It's been a family favorite ever since! I like to serve it with crusty French bread. If you double the recipe, don't double the flour... it makes the soup way too thick!

6 T. butter
1/3 c. all-purpose flour
3 c. chicken broth
1 c. milk
1 c. cooked chicken, chopped

1/8 t. pepper
1 to 2 c. cooked wild rice
Optional: snipped fresh parsley,
  diced pimentos

Melt butter in a large saucepan over medium heat; bend in flour. Slowly stir in chicken broth and milk. Cook and stir until mixture thickens and comes to a boil. Reduce heat to medium-low; stir in chicken and pepper. Heat again just to boiling. Just before serving, stir in cooked rice. Garnish with snipped parsley and pimentos, if desired. Makes 6 servings.

Autumn weather can be so fickle, chilly one moment, then balmy the next...so keep some apple cider on hand. Whether it's served chilled or spiced and piping-hot, it's always refreshing.

Parmesan Zucchini Bread

Paula Marchesi
Auburn, PA

One of my favorites. I look forward to fall, with cooler weather and colorful landscapes. It's a great time of year to do some baking! Parmesan cheese pairs well with zucchini in this tasty recipe.

3 c. all-purpose flour
3 T. plus 2 t. grated Parmesan
   cheese, divided
1 t. salt
1/2 t. baking powder
1/2 t. baking soda
2 eggs, room temperature

1 c. buttermilk
1/3 c. sugar
1/3 c. butter, melted and
   slightly cooled
1 c. zucchini, shredded
1- 1/2 T. onion, finely chopped

In a large bowl, combine flour, 3 tablespoons Parmesan cheese, salt, baking powder and baking soda; set aside. In another bowl, whisk together eggs, buttermilk, sugar and butter. Add to flour mixture; stir just until moistened. Fold in zucchini and onion. Pour batter into a greased and floured 9"x5" loaf pan. Sprinkle remaining Parmesan cheese over batter. Bake at 350 degrees for one hour, or until a toothpick inserted in the center comes out clean. Set pan on a wire rack and cool for 10 minutes. Turn loaf out of pan onto wire rack. Serve warm or cooled. Makes one loaf.

Aged Parmesan cheese is most flavorful when it's freshly grated. chunk of Parmesan will stay fresh in the fridge for several weeks if wrapped in a paper towel dampened with cider vinegar and then tucked into a plastic zipping bag.

Chilly-Day
Soups & Breads

Tasty Ranch Biscuits

Amy Thomason Hunt
Traphill, NC

*These biscuits go well with just about any dinner menu. Try them for
a change to your regular biscuit recipe...I'm sure you'll enjoy them!*

2 c. biscuit baking mix
4 t. ranch salad dressing mix
2/3 c. milk

2 T. butter, melted
1 t. dried parsley
1/8 t. garlic powder

In a bowl, combine biscuit mix, salad dressing mix and milk; stir until
well blended. Drop batter by tablespoonfuls onto a greased baking
sheet. Bake at 425 degrees for 10 to 15 minutes, until golden. Combine
butter and seasonings until well blended; brush over warm biscuits.
Makes 8 to 10 biscuits.

Easy Drop Biscuits

Jess Brunink
Whitehall, MI

*My kids love these little biscuits with stew, or right out of the oven
with a little honey. They are quick & easy! They are also great
topped with sausage gravy for breakfast.*

3 c. self-rising flour
1/2 c. butter, melted
1 c. milk or water

1/4 t. salt
1 t. sugar

Combine all ingredients in a bowl; mix well. Drop dough by
tablespoonfuls onto a greased baking sheet. Bake at 375 degrees
for 10 to 15 minutes, until golden. Makes 2 dozen.

An old-fashioned bread box
makes a handy storage place in
the pantry for seasoning mix
packets and other small items.

Loaded Baked Potato Soup

Laura Justice
Indianapolis, IN

A perfect soup for a chilly day! This is a great soup to make ahead. It actually tastes better after sitting in the fridge for a day. Just reheat, add toppings and serve....a wonderful meal for a busy night!

7 potatoes, peeled and diced
10-3/4 oz. can Cheddar
    cheese soup
12-oz. can evaporated milk
10-3/4 oz. can chicken broth,
    divided
4 c. whole milk
16-oz. pkg. shredded Cheddar
    cheese, divided

2 T. cornstarch
2 T. butter, sliced
1/2 t. onion powder
1/2 t. garlic salt
1/2 t. salt
1/2 t. pepper
Garnish: sour cream, crumbled
    bacon, chopped fresh chives

In a large saucepan, cover potatoes with water. Bring to a boil over high heat; cook until fork-tender. Drain and set aside. Meanwhile, in a large soup pot, combine cheese soup, evaporated milk and half of chicken broth. Cook over medium heat, whisking until smooth. Stir in whole milk and shredded cheese, reserving 1/2 cup cheese for garnish. Cook and whisk until cheese is melted. Add cornstarch to remaining broth; mix well and add to soup pot. Add butter and seasonings. Bring to a boil; reduce heat to medium-low. Simmer for 15 to 20 minutes, stirring often. Add potatoes and simmer another 15 minutes. Garnish with reserved cheese and other toppings, as desired. Makes 8 servings.

A muffin tin is handy when you're serving lots of tasty toppings. Fill up the sections with shredded cheese, crumbled bacon, sour cream and whatever you like...let everyone mix & match their favorites!

Chilly-Day
Soups & Breads

Hunter's Best Vegetable Soup

Sarah Slaven
Strunk, KY

This is the best fall soup! My husband loves to come home to this soup after a chilly day out hunting. It is delicious made with venison as well.

1-1/2 lbs. ground beef
1 onion, chopped
5 c. beef broth
1 T. garlic powder
1 T. seasoned salt

1 to 2 14-1/2 oz. cans diced
   fire-roasted tomatoes
15-1/2 oz. can mixed vegetables
14-oz. can corn

Brown beef with onion in a large soup pot over medium heat; drain. Add beef broth and seasonings; simmer for about 15 minutes. Add tomatoes, mixed vegetables and corn; do not drain any cans. Bring to a boil; reduce heat to low. Simmer for 45 minutes to one hour, stirring occasionally. Serves 6.

Carve swirling designs in pumpkins using a linoleum craft knife. Since only the outer surface is carved, there's no need to hollow out the pumpkins...so easy!

Creamy Butternut Squash Soup

Barb Bargdill
Gooseberry Patch

I like to welcome my Thanksgiving guests with cups of this delicious, creamy soup. Frozen squash certainly save on cooking time! Garnish with a dollop of sour cream and a little cinnamon.

1/4 c. butter
2 10-oz. pkgs. frozen diced
    butternut squash, thawed
2 Granny Smith apples, peeled,
    cored and diced
3/4 c. onion, diced

5 c. vegetable broth
14-oz. can coconut milk
1 t. kosher salt
1/2 t. dried sage
1/2 t. cinnamon

Melt butter in a large saucepan over medium heat; add squash, apples and onion. Sauté for about 10 minutes, until apples begin to soften. Stir in remaining ingredients; bring to a boil. Reduce heat to medium-low; simmer for 45 minutes, or until apples are tender. Purée soup with an immersion blender until smooth, or allow soup to cool and process in a blender. Makes 4 to 6 servings.

Why not get out Mom's soup tureen set for cozy soup dinners with your family? The ladle makes serving easy and the lid keeps soup piping hot and steamy...perfect!

Family-
Favorite
Comfort Foods

Welcome AUTUMN

Slow-Cooker Autumn Beans & 'Basa

Laura Witham
Anchorage, AK

There's nothing better than a crisp autumn morning...except the aroma of the slow cooker cooking up an awesome batch of beans! Start these the night before and by lunchtime, all you have to do is enjoy autumn and a yummy bowl of Beans & 'Basa! Serve with cornbread for a real treat.

16-oz. pkg dried mixed beans, rinsed and sorted
14-1/2 oz. can petite diced tomatoes
1 lb. Kielbasa sausage, diced

1 to 2 carrots, peeled and diced
8 c. beef broth
2 T. Cajun seasoning
1 T. onion powder
2 t. garlic powder

Add dried beans to a 5-quart slow cooker; reserve seasoning packet for another use. Stir in tomatoes with juice and remaining ingredients. Cover and cook on low setting for 8 to 12 hours, or on high setting for 6 hours, stirring occasionally. Makes 6 to 8 servings.

Have a back-to-school dinner especially for the kids...
set a table outside and serve up all their favorite foods.
A great way to make memories!

Family-Favorite
Comfort Foods

Cheeseburger Macaroni Skillet

Tina Wright
Atlanta, GA

My grandkids are always busy with school activities in fall. With this recipe, I can stir up a hearty meal that they love...no need to precook the macaroni! Substitute cavatappi pasta for twisty fun.

1 lb. lean ground beef
8-oz. pkg. elbow macaroni, uncooked
3 c. reduced-sodium beef broth
3/4 c. milk
3 T. catsup

2 t. Montreal steak seasoning
1 t. mustard
1/4 t. onion powder
Optional: pepper to taste
1 c. shredded Cheddar cheese

Brown beef in a large skillet over medium heat, breaking up beef with a spatula; drain. Stir in uncooked macaroni and remaining ingredients except cheese; bring to a boil. Reduce heat to medium-low. Simmer for 10 to 15 minutes, until macaroni is tender. Add cheese; stir until melted and serve. Serves 6.

Welcoming table decor in a jiffy! Tuck votives into Mason jars and set them down the center of the table. Surround the jars with mini pumpkins, gourds, berry twigs and colorful leaves... oh-so pretty!

Welcome AUTUMN

Pumpkin Marinara with Italian Sausage

Laurie Malone
Wheeling, IL

Pumpkin is good for you! Last Halloween, I used specialty pasta shaped like pumpkins and bats, just for fun. Even though pumpkin is considered an autumn ingredient, this is tasty all year. Sometimes I add some diced cooked chicken breast to this recipe.

16-oz. pkg. cavatappi or bowtie
   pasta, uncooked
1 lb. ground mild Italian
   pork sausage
28-oz. can petite diced
   tomatoes, drained
24-oz. jar marinara sauce

15-oz. can pumpkin
6-oz. can tomato paste
Italian seasoning, salt and pepper
   to taste
Garnish: shredded Parmesan
   cheese

Cook pasta according to package directions; drain. Meanwhile, brown sausage in a skillet over medium heat, breaking it into small pieces as it cooks. When sausage is nearly done, stir in remaining ingredients except garnish. Simmer until sausage is fully cooked and sauce is bubbly. Serve sausage and sauce over hot pasta, with shredded Parmesan cheese on top. Makes 6 to 8 servings.

Thanksgiving Day is a terrific time to catch up on the past year with family & friends. Set up a family memory table and ask everybody to bring along snapshots, clippings, even crafts... you'll all have so much to talk about!

Family-Favorite
Comfort Foods

Sausages in Batter

Diane Bertosa
Brunswick Hills, OH

I have been making this tasty dish for over 50 years, so you know it's good. Sausages bake in a crisp, puffy and golden batter. It is so easy yet so delicious, a family favorite! We usually enjoy this simple yet substantial dish with cinnamon-flavored applesauce...a fruit salad might be nice too.

12-oz. pkg. pork breakfast
   sausage links
3/4 c. milk
2 eggs, beaten

3/4 c. all-purpose flour
1 T. butter, melted
1/2 t. salt
1/4 t. pepper

In a large skillet over medium heat, cook sausages until lightly browned; drain. Arrange sausages in a 9"x9" baking pan coated with non-stick vegetable spray; set aside. Combine remaining ingredients in a bowl; beat until smooth. Pour batter over sausages in pan. Bake, uncovered, at 400 degrees for 30 minutes, or until batter is puffed, crisp and golden. Makes 6 to 8 servings.

Short Rib Supper

Monty Rae Miles
Medford, OR

A hearty meal in one pan! Worcestershire sauce can be used instead of teriyaki sauce. Serve with dinner rolls and coleslaw.

3 lbs. boneless beef short ribs
3/4 c. onion, chopped
3 c. water
3 T. teriyaki sauce
2 t. paprika

2 t. salt
1/4 t. pepper
2 potatoes, peeled and cut
   into chunks
1/2 c. pearled barley, uncooked

In a Dutch oven, combine short ribs, onion, water, teriyaki sauce and seasonings. Bring to a boil over medium-high heat. Reduce heat to low; cover and cook for 1-1/2 hours, stirring occasionally. Add potatoes and barley. Cover and cook for an additional hour, stirring occasionally and adding more water if necessary. Serves 4.

Jim's Kielbasa Vegetable Stew

Carolyn Deckard
Bedford, IN

My husband Jim remembers his mom making this great stew using vegetables from her own garden. Now he makes the stew for our family. He leaves the peel on the potatoes and cuts the vegetables into large pieces, says it's faster that way!

1 red onion, cut into thin wedges
14-1/2 oz. can stewed tomatoes, drained
6 new redskin potatoes, cut into quarters
1 c. carrots, peeled and cut into 2-1/4 inch strips

1/2 lb. Kielbasa sausage, sliced 1/2-inch thick
1 t. fresh marjoram, chopped, or 1/4 t. dried marjoram
1/8 t. pepper
2 c. cabbage, coarsely chopped

Spray a large non-stick skillet with non-stick vegetable spray; heat over medium heat. Cook onion in skillet for 2 to 3 minutes, stirring occasionally, until tender-crisp. Stir in remaining ingredients except cabbage; bring to a boil. Reduce heat to medium-low. Cover and cook for 10 minutes. Stir in cabbage. Cover and cook for 5 to 10 minutes, stirring occasionally, until vegetables are tender. Makes 4 to 6 servings.

Haunt the porch steps with ghostly Jack-o'Lanterns... simply choose white pumpkins for carving!

Family-Favorite
Comfort Foods

Cheesy-Peasy Smoked Sausage Casserole

Angela Bissette
Wilson, NC

One day I was craving comfort food and came up with this recipe. It is simple to prepare, delicious and very filling.

7-1/2 oz. pkg. macaroni & cheese mix
2 T. olive oil
1 lb. smoked beef, pork or turkey sausage, sliced
3/4 c. onion, diced
1 c. sliced mushrooms
2 T. garlic, minced
2 c. frozen peas, thawed
Garnish: shredded Cheddar cheese

Prepare macaroni mix according to package directions. Meanwhile, heat oil in a skillet over medium heat. Add sausage, onion, mushrooms and garlic. Cook until sausage is browned and onion is tender, about 10 minutes. Remove from heat. Add peas and macaroni & cheese; mix well. Spread mixture in a greased 13"x9" baking pan; top with cheese as desired. Bake, uncovered, at 350 degrees for 15 to 20 minutes, until hot and bubbly. Makes 8 servings.

Take it easy on alternate Friday nights...arrange for a friendly dinner swap! One week, you make a double batch of a favorite casserole and deliver one to a friend. Next week, she returns the favor. You're sure to discover some great new recipes while gaining a littlc free time too.

Welcome AUTUMN

Chicken Cordon Bleu Pasta

Joyce Hurt
Shreve, OH

My sister and I always looked for easy ways to make dishes we enjoyed. I found this scrumptious recipe and it's so much easier to make than the usual way...a big hit for both our families!

2 c. penne pasta, uncooked
2 c. whipping cream
8-oz. pkg. cream cheese, softened and cubed
1/2 t. onion powder
1/2 t. garlic salt
1/4 t. pepper

1-1/2 c. shredded Swiss cheese, divided
3 c. cooked chicken breast, sliced
3/4 c. bacon, crisply cooked and crumbled
3/4 c. cooked ham, cubed
3 T. dry bread crumbs

Cook pasta according to package directions, just until tender; drain. Meanwhile, in a large saucepan, combine cream and cream cheese. Cook over medium heat until smooth, stirring occasionally; do not boil. Stir in seasonings and one cup shredded cheese until blended. In a large bowl, combine chicken, bacon, ham and cooked pasta. Add sauce; toss to coat. Transfer mixture to a greased 13"x9" baking pan. Sprinkle with remaining cheese; top with bread crumbs. Bake, uncovered, at 350 degrees for 18 to 22 minutes, until heated through. Makes 6 to 8 servings.

Dinner :
Roast Turkey
Mashed Potatoes
Apple Crisp

Show off the Thanksgiving menu in a rustic frame. Select several straight twigs and tie together at the corners with jute. Decorate the corners with tiny acorns.

Family-Favorite
Comfort Foods

Pepper & Onion Rice

Caroline Timbs
Cord, AR

This recipe is very versatile and can't be messed up! I created it when our garden was overflowing with a variety of peppers. It has been a favorite ever since. We enjoy it as a meatless main, served with garden okra and baby carrots. It's also good with some cooked chicken breast chunks added and a big tossed salad on the side.

1/2 c. butter, divided
2 green peppers, chopped
2 red peppers, chopped
5 assorted mini sweet
   peppers, chopped
1 onion, chopped

1 c. chicken broth
1 T. chicken bouillon granules
2 c. cooked rice
3 T. Greek seasoning
1/4 c. dry bread crumbs
1/4 c. grated Parmesan cheese

Melt one tablespoon butter in a large skillet over medium heat. Add all peppers and onion; sauté until tender. Add remaining butter, chicken broth and bouillon; heat through. Add cooked rice and mix until well coated. Add seasoning; mix well and heat through. Top with bread crumbs and Parmesan cheese; serve. Serves 8.

Chicken Diablo

Denise Bushnell
Clifton, VA

Despite its name, this is not a spicy dish. It is always a family favorite...a great dish to bring to a sick friend, freezes well and doubles easily. The sauce is delicious spooned over rice!

3 lbs. boneless or bone-in
   chicken pieces
1/4 c. butter

1/2 c. honey
1/4 c. mustard
1 t. curry powder

Arrange chicken pieces in a lightly greased 13"x9" baking pan; set aside. Melt butter in a small saucepan over medium heat. Add remaining ingredients; blend well. Add sauce to chicken; coat well. Bake, uncovered, at 350 degrees for about 30 minutes if boneless, or 45 to 60 minutes, if bone-in. Makes 4 servings.

Welcome AUTUMN

Faye's Cracker Crumb Chicken

Debbie Adkins
Nicholasville, KY

My mom often made this wonderful baked chicken when I was growing up in the 50s and 60s, and it's still one of my favorites. She always used saltine crackers, but you can also use a buttery cracker if you prefer.

2 eggs, lightly beaten
1-1/4 c. saltine crackers, crushed
4 boneless, skinless chicken
    breasts

1/2 c. butter, thinly sliced

Beat eggs in a shallow dish; add cracker crumbs to another dish. Dip chicken pieces in beaten egg, then roll in cracker crumbs until completely coated. Arrange chicken on an aluminum foil-lined rimmed baking sheet. Lay butter slices on top of chicken so each piece is covered. Bake, uncovered, at 375 degrees for about 40 minutes, until thickest part of chicken is done and juices run clear when pierced. Serves 4.

Sweet & Spicy Chicken Thighs

Sandy Ward
Anderson, IN

Oh-so easy...and oh-so tasty!

10 to 12 boneless, skinless
    chicken thighs
3 T. chili powder

3 T. honey
2 T. lemon juice
salt and pepper to taste

Arrange chicken in a 15"x10" jelly-roll pan lined with heavy-duty aluminum foil; set aside. Combine remaining ingredients in a cup; brush over chicken, turning to coat completely. Bake, uncovered, at 425 degrees for 45 minutes, turning once, or until chicken juices run clear when pieced. Serves 5 to 6, 2 pieces each.

Roll up homespun napkins, tie with ribbon bows and slip
a sprig of bittersweet under the ribbons...simple!

Family-Favorite
Comfort Foods

Skillet Stuffing Casserole

Jennifer Murphy
Denver, CO

I just love Thanksgiving stuffing! I wanted a casserole that was reminiscent of it, and these were the ingredients I had on hand. It's baked in the skillet, so there aren't many dishes to wash.

8-1/2 oz. pkg. cornbread mix
1 lb. ground pork sausage
   with sage
10-3/4 oz. can cream of
   chicken soup

15-oz. can corn, drained
1/2 c. shredded Cheddar cheese
salt and pepper to taste

Prepare cornbread mix according to package directions, using a little less liquid than called for; set aside batter. Brown sausage in an oven-safe skillet over medium heat; drain and return sausage to pan. Remove from heat; stir in remaining ingredients. Spoon batter over sausage mixture, covering as much as possible. Place skillet in oven. Bake, uncovered, at 350 degrees for 25 minutes, or until cornbread is golden. Carefully remove from oven and serve. Makes 4 to 6 servings.

Begin a new Thanksgiving tradition. Before dinner, take time to hold hands and ask everyone at the table to share what they're thankful for...some of the sweetest memories will be made.

Pork-Stuffed Acorn Squash

Diane Hixon
Niceville, FL

Whenever I think of fall, this recipe comes to mind. I love any type
of squash! Lean ground beef can be used instead of pork.

3 small acorn squash, halved
   and seeds removed
1/2 c. water
1 lb. ground pork
3/4 c. dry bread crumbs
3/4 c. onion, minced

1 egg, beaten
1/2 c. Russian or Catalina salad
   dressing
1 T. brown sugar, packed
1 t. lemon juice
3/4 t. salt

Place squash halves in an ungreased roasting pan, cut-side down; pour
water around squash. Bake, uncovered, at 350 degrees for 30 minutes.
Meanwhile, combine remaining ingredients in a large bowl; mix well and
set aside. Remove squash from oven and turn cut-side up; increase oven
temperature to 375 degrees. Spoon filling into squash halves. Brush
Glaze over filling and top of squash. Bake, uncovered, at 375 degrees
for 40 to 50 minutes, brushing with glaze every 15 minutes. Serves 6.

Glaze:

1/4 c. Russian or Catalina
   salad dressing

1-1/2 t. brown sugar, packed
1-1/2 t. lemon juice

Combine all ingredients; mix well.

Use a grapefruit spoon or melon baller to scoop out
the seeds from squash or pumpkin...so easy!

Family-Favorite
Comfort Foods

Rustic Chicken, Pesto & Artichoke Pasta

Terry Felder
Sorrento, FL

We came up with this recipe after returning home from a trip to Italy. Many days on our vacation, we stopped at a local Italian grocery store and picked up ingredients for a picnic lunch overlooking the Italian Riviera. This dish features a few of the wonderful flavors of Italy without having to travel overseas! It always gets rave reviews. Break open a fresh baguette, serve with a crisp salad and savor dinner the way it should be.

16-oz. pkg. linguine pasta,
   uncooked
1-1/2 c. whipping cream
8.1-oz. jar pesto sauce
1 deli rotisserie chicken,
   shredded
7-oz. jar sun-dried tomatoes
   in oil

14-oz. can quartered artichokes,
   drained
1 c. pine nuts
3/4 c. grated Parmesan cheese
1/2 t. lemon juice
Garnish: chopped fresh parsley

Cook pasta according to package directions; drain and return to pan. Meanwhile, in a saucepan over medium heat, combine cream and pesto sauce. Cook and stir until blended together and thickened. Add to cooked pasta along with remaining ingredients except garnish. Stir until pasta is coated with sauce. Top with chopped parsley and serve. Makes 4 to 6 servings.

I awoke this morning with devout thanksgiving for
my friends, the old and new.
–Ralph Waldo Emerson

Slow-Cooker Brisket

Angie Miller
Wichita Falls, TX

This was my great-grandmother's recipe. Over the years, I've adjusted and played with it...I hope you'll agree it's wonderful.

4 to 5-lb. beef brisket
3 t. garlic powder, divided
2 t. chili powder
1/2 t. paprika
2 t. salt
2 t. pepper

1/2 c. catsup
1/3 c. cider vinegar
1/4 c. brown sugar, packed
2 T. Worcestershire sauce
2 t. Dijon mustard

Pat brisket dry; place in a 6-quart slow cooker and set aside. In a cup, combine 2 teaspoons garlic powder, chili powder, paprika, salt and pepper; rub onto brisket. In a small bowl, whisk together remaining garlic powder and other ingredients; spoon over brisket. Cover and cook on low setting for 7 to 8 hours, until brisket is very tender. Remove to a platter; slice and serve. Serves 4 to 6.

Bundukis

Dawn Byers
Grand Forks, ND

My family loves this recipe for tasty bacon and beef-filled buns! We enjoy it with barbecue beans, or just by itself.

12 frozen dinner rolls
14-oz. pkg. bacon, cut into
    1-inch pieces
1 lb. ground beef
dried, minced onions to taste

salt-free seasoning or salt and
    pepper to taste
8-oz. pkg. shredded mozzarella
    cheese
1 T. dried parsley

Thaw dinner rolls according to package directions. Meanwhile, cook bacon in a skillet over medium heat until crisp; set aside on paper towels. Drain most of drippings in skillet. Add beef and cook until browned. Add onions and seasoning as desired; drain. Add bacon, cheese and parsley to beef; mix well. Stretch and flatten each roll. Fill with beef mixture and pinch seams together. Place buns seam-side down in a greased 13"x9" baking pan. Bake at 350 degrees for 20 to 25 minutes, until lightly golden. Makes one dozen.

Family-Favorite
Comfort Foods

Herbed Pork Tenderloins

Janet Ambruster
Apex, NC

Always a hit! These tenderloins are easy and so delicious. Pop a tray of roasted vegetables in the oven too, for a complete meal.

2 3/4 to 1-lb. pork tenderloins
1 c. low-sodium soy sauce
2 cloves garlic, minced
2 T. lemon juice
2 t. dried basil

2 t. dried tarragon
1 t. dried chives
1 t. ground sage
1 t. pepper

Place tenderloins in a resealable plastic zipping bag; set aside. Mix together remaining ingredients in a bowl; pour into bag. Seal and turn bag to coat pork. Refrigerate for 8 hours or overnight, turning bag occasionally. Remove tenderloins from bag and place in a lightly greased 13"x9" baking pan. Pour marinade from bag into a saucepan and bring to a boil for 3 minutes; drizzle over tenderloins. Cover pan with aluminum foil. Bake at 350 degrees for 45 to 60 minutes, until a meat thermometer inserted in thickest part reads 145 degrees. Remove tenderloins to a platter; allow to rest 15 minutes before slicing. Makes 4 to 6 servings.

ooompah!

Host a backyard Oktoberfest party! Set a festive mood with polka music. Toss some brats on the grill to serve in hard rolls, topped with sauerkraut. Round out the menu with potato salad, homemade applesauce and German chocolate cake for dessert. It's sure to be a good time for all.

Cheesy Chicken–Stuffed Poblano Peppers

Constance Bockstoce
Dallas, GA

One day I was given several large poblano peppers, but had no idea what to do with them, I decided to do a stuffed pepper with a spicy twist. The Mexican flavors were quite a hit with my 94-year-old father and my 27-year-old son. Some of the peppers will have blackened spots. Don't worry...they taste delicious!

6 large poblano peppers, tops
  cut off, halved and seeds
  removed
3 c. deli rotisserie chicken,
  finely diced
10-oz. can diced tomatoes with
  green chiles, drained

8-oz. pkg. shredded Mexican-
  blend cheese
1/2 c. salsa
2 t. taco seasoning mix
6 to 8 slices Pepper Jack cheese

Place pepper halves on a parchment paper-lined baking sheet, cut-side up; set aside. In a large bowl, combine remaining ingredients except cheese slices; mix well, using your hands. Generously fill pepper halves with chicken mixture. Bake, uncovered, at 400 degrees for 30 minutes. Remove from oven; top each pepper with 1/2 to one cheese slice. Return to oven for 3 minutes, or until cheese is melted. Let stand 5 minutes and serve. Make 6 to 8 servings.

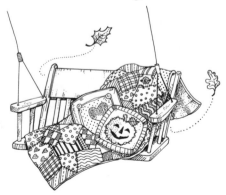

Make the most of your front porch! A porch swing, rocking chairs, comfy pillows and hanging baskets of fall flowers create a cozy place for family & friends to visit and enjoy the crisp air.

Family-Favorite
Comfort Foods

Jalapeño Popper Casserole

Amanda Rentiers
Winnsboro, SC

A great weeknight casserole...just add a basket of crispy tortilla chips for crunch! To make ahead, prepare, wrap well and freeze unbaked up to eight weeks. Thaw in fridge and bake as directed.

12-oz. pkg. wide egg noodles, uncooked
2 8-oz. pkgs. cream cheese, softened
1-oz. pkg. ranch salad dressing mix
1 c. sour cream

1/2 c. milk
4 jalapeño peppers, halved, seeds removed and diced
1-1/2 c. cooked chicken, chopped or shredded
8-oz. pkg. shredded Cheddar cheese, divided

Cook noodles according to package directions; drain. Meanwhile, in a large bowl, blend cream cheese, salad dressing mix, sour cream and milk. Stir in peppers, chicken and one cup shredded cheese. Add noodles; mix well and spread in a greased 13"x9" baking pan. Top with remaining cheese. Bake, uncovered, at 350 degrees for 20 to 25 minutes, until hot and bubbly. Serves 6 to 8.

Slow-Cooker Chili Verde

Sharalee Plaku
Dallas, OR

I made up this recipe for a quick meal my family loves. I serve it with steamed rice and tortillas.

1 to 1-1/2 lbs. stew beef cubes
1/4 c. sliced pickled jalapeño peppers
15-oz. can green enchilada sauce

2 T. garlic, minced
1 t. chili powder
1/2 t. ground cumin
1/4 t. dried Mexican oregano

Combine beef cubes and peppers in a 4-quart slow cooker; set aside. Combine remaining ingredients in a bowl; spoon over beef mixture. Cover and cook on low setting for 7 to 8 hours. Serves 6.

Delicious Brined Turkey Breast

Megan Brooks
Antioch, TN

*Brining a turkey breast isn't really difficult...and your guests
will be so impressed by this juicy bird!*

8 c. water
1 c. dry white wine or water
1/2 c. plus 1/2 t. salt, divided
1/2 c. sugar
4 bay leaves
5 to 6-lb. bone-in turkey breast,
    thawed if frozen

1 to 2 T. oil
1 t. paprika
1/2 t. dried rosemary
1/2 t. dried thyme

In a 6-quart stockpot or other deep container, combine 8 cups water,
wine or water, 1/2 cup salt, sugar and bay leaves. Stir until salt and
sugar dissolve. Add turkey breast to brine; set a plate on top to keep it
covered in brine, if necessary. Refrigerate for 12 to 24 hours. Remove
turkey from brine and rinse with cool water; discard brine. Pat dry with
paper towels. Place on a rack in an aluminum foil-lined roasting pan;
brush with oil. Mix herbs and remaining salt in a cup; sprinkle evenly
over turkey. Cover loosely with aluminum foil. Bake at 325 degrees
for one hour; uncover. Bake, uncovered, for one to 1-1/2 hours longer,
until a meat thermometer inserted in the thickest part reads 165 degrees.
Baste occasionally with pan juices. Remove turkey to a serving platter.
Cover loosely and let stand 15 minutes; slice and serve. Serves 10.

For dark, rich-looking gravy, add a spoonful or 2 of brewed black
coffee. It will add color to pale gravy, but won't affect the flavor.

Family-Favorite
Comfort Foods

Cranberry-Barbecue Turkey Sandwiches

Katherine Wollgast
Troy, MO

When I slice those holiday turkeys, I always have some little scraps that just aren't pretty enough for the platter. Thanks to this recipe, I now try to get more of those scraps! This is my absolute favorite turkey sandwich. I like these for lunch or light dinner on pretzel buns. For less mess and a true feast, serve open-face over thick toasted bread or leftover stuffing, with mashed potatoes and gravy on the side.

14-oz. can whole-berry
   cranberry sauce
1 T. Worcestershire sauce
1/4 c. barbecue sauce
1 c. beef broth
2 T. cider vinegar
1 t. mustard
1/4 t. garlic powder
1/2 t. seasoned salt
1/8 t. smoked paprika

6 c. roast turkey, shredded
1 T. cornstarch
2 T. cold water
12 sandwich buns, split and
   warmed or toasted
light mayonnaise-style salad
   dressing to taste
Optional: 12 slices Swiss cheese,
   3 c. creamy coleslaw

In a large saucepan, combine all sauces, beef broth, vinegar, mustard and seasonings. Mix well; fold in turkey. Bring to a boil over medium-high heat. Reduce heat to low; cover and simmer for 5 minutes. Mix together cornstarch and water in a cup; add to mixture in pan. Cook and stir until sauce is slightly thickened. At serving time, spread cut sides of buns with salad dressing. Fill each bun with 1/2 cup turkey mixture. If desired, top each with one slice cheese and 1/4 cup coleslaw. Cover with bun tops and serve immediately. Makes 12 sandwiches.

Serve up sweet potato fries with sandwiches. Slice sweet potatoes into wedges, toss with olive oil and bake at 400 degrees for 20 to 30 minutes, turning once, until tender. Sprinkle with cinnamon-sugar and serve warm.

Chicago–Style Pan Pizza

Jill Burton
Gooseberry Patch

By the end of Thanksgiving weekend, we're getting pretty tired of turkey leftovers. This pizza is a great change of pace!

1-lb. loaf frozen bread dough
1 lb. ground Italian pork sausage
1/2 c. onion, chopped
8-oz. pkg. shredded Italian-blend cheese
1/2 lb. sliced mushrooms
2 t. olive oil

28-oz. can diced tomatoes, drained
3/4 t. dried oregano
1/2 t. fennel seed, crushed
1/2 t. salt
1/4 t. garlic powder
1/2 c. grated Parmesan cheese

Thaw dough according to package directions. Press into the bottom and up the sides of a greased 13"x9" baking pan; set aside. In a large skillet over medium heat, brown sausage with onion; drain. Spread sausage mixture over dough; top with Italian-blend cheese. In same skillet, sauté mushrooms in oil until tender. Stir in tomatoes and seasonings; spoon over sausage. Sprinkle with Parmesan cheese. Bake, uncovered, at 350 degrees for 25 to 35 minutes, until bubbly and crust is golden. Cut into squares. Serves 6.

For an easy meal on a busy day, serve up a slider bar with shredded chicken, pulled pork, baskets of buns and lots of condiments.

Family-Favorite
Comfort Foods

Fiesta Tots

Amanda Walton
Marysville, OH

This recipe is my version of a dish that we had while on vacation at our favorite amusement park. We all loved it, and were thrilled to have it again at home. It's basically nachos with a twist.

32-oz. pkg frozen potato puffs
1 T. oil
3/4 c. onion, chopped
1 red or green pepper, chopped
1 lb. lean ground beef
1/4 c. chicken broth or water
3 T. taco seasoning mix
2 T. butter
2 T. all-purpose flour
1 to 2 c. milk, warmed and divided
1-1/2 c. shredded Pepper Jack cheese
1/2 c. shredded Mexican-blend cheese
salt to taste
Garnish: sour cream, pico de gallo, guacamole

Bake potato puffs according to package directions. Meanwhile, heat oil in a large skillet over medium heat. Sauté onion and pepper for 5 minutes, or until softened. Add beef and cook until browned; drain. Stir in chicken broth or water and taco seasoning. Simmer, covered, for 20 minutes. Make cheese sauce. Melt butter in a saucepan over medium heat; whisk in flour. Cook, stirring constantly, for about 3 to 5 minutes, until mixture is golden and smells nutty. Slowly whisk in one cup warmed milk. Allow to simmer and thicken for a few minutes. Slowly add both cheeses, a handful at a time, allowing cheese to fully melt before adding next batch. Add more milk, if desired, to achieve desired consistency. Season with salt. Keep cheese sauce over low heat while assembling servings. To serve, divide potato puffs evenly among 6 shallow bowls. Top each with a spoonful of beef mixture, then a spoonful of cheese sauce; add desired toppings. Makes 6 servings.

Let the kids invite a special friend or two home for dinner.
Keep it simple with a hearty casserole and a relish tray of crunchy veggies & dip. A great way to get to know your children's playmates!

Cod & Potato Bake

Melina Sarnese
Ontario, Canada

Mom used to make this casserole for us on Fridays. It is a comforting dish, filling the house with the delicious scents of lemon, garlic, oregano and parsley.

1 whole lemon
4 4-oz. cod fillets, thawed
   if frozen
4 russet potatoes, peeled and
   quartered lengthwise
1 onion, sliced
1/4 c. extra-virgin olive oil
1/4 c. white wine or water

1 T. fresh Italian parsley, minced
2 cloves garlic, minced
1 t. dried oregano
1/8 t. cayenne pepper
salt and pepper to taste
1/4 c. butter, melted
1/4 c. panko bread crumbs

Grate zest from lemon; squeeze juice from lemon and set aside. Layer fish fillets, potatoes and onion in a parchment paper-lined 3-quart casserole dish. Drizzle with reserved lemon juice, olive oil and wine or water; sprinkle with parsley, garlic and seasonings. Toss to coat fish and vegetables; set aside. In a bowl, combine reserved lemon zest, melted butter and panko crumbs; season with additional salt and pepper. Sprinkle crumb mixture over fish and vegetables. Bake, uncovered, at 375 degrees for 40 minutes, or until potatoes are crisp and golden. Makes 4 servings.

Slip children's drawings between 2 pieces of clear self-adhesive plastic for placemats that are both practical and playful... sure to tickle grandparents!

Family-Favorite
Comfort Foods

3-Cheese Stuffed Shells

Tiffany Jones
Batesville, AR

I am a big fan of pasta! This is a simple recipe that I enjoy making on cool, crisp fall afternoons while my twins play with homemade play clay. While it's baking, I join in on the fun, then we all have a yummy family dinner together.

12-oz. pkg jumbo pasta shells,
   uncooked
15-oz. container ricotta cheese
1-1/2 c. grated Parmesan cheese
1 c. shredded mozzarella cheese
1 egg, beaten

1 T. dried parsley
1 T. dried oregano
salt and pepper to taste
1 to 2 24-oz. jars spaghetti
   sauce, divided

Cook pasta shells according to package directions; drain and rinse. Meanwhile, in a plastic zipping bag, combine cheeses, eggs and seasonings. Squeeze together until thoroughly combined. To assemble, spread a small amount of spaghetti sauce in the bottom of a lightly greased 13"x9" baking pan. Snip one corner of bag; fill shells by squeezing bag. Arrange filled shells over sauce in pan, open-side up. Spoon remaining sauce over shells; if you like extra sauce, add another jar of sauce. Bake, uncovered, at 400 degrees for 20 minutes, or until bubbly and cheeses melt. Makes 6 servings.

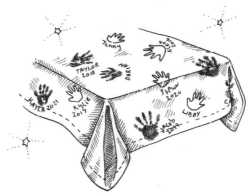

Set the table for Thanksgiving with a plain white tablecloth. Have everyone sign it with a permanent marker or, if you're crafty, in pencil to embroider later. Small children can trace their handprints. Next year, repeat...sure to become a cherished tradition!

Easy Tortellini with Spinach

Carina Furia
Wayland, NY

I love to make this slow-cooker recipe on a chilly fall day. It's perfect for watching football on Sundays, or for taking to a potluck dinner. You may also add some cubed chicken or sliced Italian sausage, if you like, partially precook before adding, to make sure the meat cooks through while baking. Serve with warm garlic bread.

2 16-oz. pkgs. frozen cheese
   tortellini, uncooked
5-oz. pkg. fresh spinach
2 14-1/2 oz. cans diced tomatoes
   with garlic
8-oz. pkg. cream cheese, cubed

2 c. chicken broth
8-oz. pkg. favorite shredded
   cheese, divided
Italian seasoning, garlic powder,
   salt and pepper to taste

In a 4-quart slow cooker, layer tortellini, spinach, tomatoes with juice and cream cheese. Pour chicken broth over all; top with one cup shredded cheese. Add seasonings as desired. Cover and cook on low setting for 4 hours, or until bubbly and tortellini is cooked through. Serve in bowls, topped with remaining cheese. Serves 6.

An oh-so-simple harvest decoration...roll out a wheelbarrow
and heap it full of large, colorful squash and pumpkins.

Family-Favorite
Comfort Foods

Baked Flounder with Panko

Anna Frioli
Belleair Beach, FL

I wanted to try a recipe that would make fish taste better to me. So I added Parmesan cheese and a pinch of dill weed and thyme, then baked it until crisp. That did the trick for me!

4 4-oz. flounder fillets, thawed
   if frozen
1/4 c. butter, melted and divided
2/3 c. grated Parmesan cheese
1 c. panko bread crumbs

1/2 t. sea salt
1/8 t. pepper
1/8 t. dried dill weed
1/8 t. dried thyme

Arrange fish fillets in a greased 13"x9" baking pan. Brush with one tablespoon melted butter; set aside. Combine remaining butter, Parmesan cheese, panko crumbs and seasonings in a small bowl. Sprinkle over fish and pat down to stick. Bake, uncovered, at 400 degrees for 25 minutes, or until flaky and crisp. Serves 4.

Lemon-Garlic Baked Fish

Linda Belon
Wintersville, OH

We ate at a local restaurant and I ordered the baked fish...it was delicious. I asked my waitress if she knew why it was so good, so she asked the chef and he told her the ingredients. I just had to figure out the amounts and time...I made it and it turned out great. A real winner!

4 4-oz. cod or tilapia fillets,
   thawed if frozen
2 T. olive oil

garlic salt and pepper to taste
3 T. lemon juice
snipped fresh dill to taste

Arrange fish fillets in a greased 13"x9" baking pan. Drizzle with olive oil; sprinkle with garlic salt and pepper. Drizzle lemon juice over fish and sprinkle with dill weed. Bake, uncovered, at 350 degrees for 20 to 30 minutes, until fish flakes easily. Serves 4.

Broccoli-Cheese Stuffed Chicken Breasts

Mel Chencharick
Julian, PA

These chicken breasts are stuffed with a yummy filling. Quick & easy...your whole family will love this!

3 boneless, skinless chicken
　　breasts
1-1/2 t. garlic powder, divided
1/4 t. paprika
salt and pepper to taste
1 c. broccoli, finely chopped

2 T. water
1/2 c. red pepper, finely chopped
1 c. shredded mild Cheddar
　　cheese
1 T. mayonnaise
2 T. olive oil

With a sharp knife, slice through the center side of each chicken breast, but not all the way through, creating a pocket. Season on both sides with 1/2 teaspoon garlic powder, paprika, salt and pepper; set aside. In a microwave-safe dish, combine broccoli and water. Cover with plastic wrap; microwave for one minute and drain. Add red pepper, shredded cheese, mayonnaise and remaining garlic powder; season with additional salt and pepper. Mix until combined. Spoon mixture into chicken breasts; fasten with wooden toothpicks, if desired. Heat oil in a large cast-iron skillet over medium heat. Add chicken breasts; cook for 3 to 4 minutes per side, until golden. Cover skillet with aluminum foil. Bake at 375 degrees for 30 minutes, or until chicken juices run clear when pierced. Let stand, covered, for 5 minutes before serving. Serves 3.

Autumn is packed with busy days. Keep a notepad on the fridge, handy for a running grocery list...no more running to the store at the last minute before starting dinner!

Family-Favorite
Comfort Foods

Grammy's Mac & Cheese

Taylor England
Clay City, IN

Growing up as a little girl, my favorite food that my Grammy made was her macaroni & cheese. I remember every time I stayed the night with her, I'd tell her she had to make it, because I loved it so much. It was really the only thing I'd even eat! It was so good that in second grade, when we had a school project of making a poster board recipe of our favorite food, my project was about her mac & cheese, of course. Now that I've grown up and moved out on my own, this is one of my comfort meals I will make if I'm having a bad day.

4 c. elbow macaroni, uncooked
1 c. milk
2 T. butter, cubed

8-oz. pkg. pasteurized process cheese, cubed

Cook macaroni according to package instructions; drain and set aside. Add milk, butter and cheese to same pan. Cook and stir over low to medium heat until cheese is melted. Return cooked macaroni back to pan. Mix together gently, until macaroni is combined with cheese sauce. Makes 6 servings.

Two sounds of autumn are unmistakable...the hurrying
rustle of crisp leaves blown along the street...by a gusty wind,
and the gabble of a flock of migrating geese.

–Hal Borland

Momma's Italian Cuisine

Kristi Powell
Butler, PA

My mom made this all the time when my brother and I were kids. Everyone loved it! I recommend serving it with a crisp tossed salad and a basket of warm garlic bread.

16-oz. pkg. spiral pasta,
    uncooked
1/4 c. shredded Parmesan cheese
1/4 c. butter
6-oz. pkg. sliced pepperoni
2 to 3 t. oil
8-oz. can mushroom pieces &
    stems, drained

1/2 c. onion, chopped
29-oz. can tomato sauce
1 T. fresh oregano, chopped
1 T. fresh parsley, chopped
1 lb. mozzarella cheese, sliced
Optional: additional mozzarella,
    Parmesan cheeses

Cook pasta according to package instruction; drain and return to pan. Add Parmesan cheese and butter; mix well and transfer to a 13"x9" baking pan. Set aside. In a skillet over medium heat, cook pepperoni in oil for 5 minutes. Add mushrooms and onion to skillet; cook for 5 minutes. Add tomato sauce and herbs to mixture in pan; cover and simmer over low heat for 15 minutes. Spread sauce mixture over cooked pasta in pan. Top with cheese slices. Cover with aluminum foil. Bake at 350 degrees for about 30 minutes, until heated through. If desired, top with additional mozzarella and Parmesan cheeses; bake 5 more minutes. Makes 8 to 10 servings.

Keep a crock of herbed garlic butter in the fridge for making garlic bread or jazzing up steamed veggies. Simply blend a teaspoon each of Italian seasoning, dried mustard and garlic powder into 1/2 cup softened butter. Yummy!

Family-Favorite
Comfort Foods

Eggplant Casserole

Mellissa Schippel
Castalia, OH

My mother began making this dish in the 1980s after she saw a chef on TV make something similar, and it quickly became one of my favorites. The original recipe called for spreading the filling on each eggplant strip and then rolling it up, but I changed the recipe to an easier layered casserole. Either way it's prepared, it is still delicious!

1 to 2 T. oil
1 eggplant, peeled and cut
   into strips
1 lb. ground pork sausage

8-oz. pkg. cream cheese,
   softened and cubed
26-oz. jar pasta sauce, divided
1 c. shredded mozzarella cheese

Add oil to a skillet over medium heat. Cook eggplant strips for 2 to 3 minutes on each side, until limp but not browned. Remove from heat. In another skillet over medium heat, cook sausage until no longer pink; drain. Add cream cheese to sausage; mix well. To assemble, spread a small amount of pasta sauce in the bottom of a lightly greased 13"x9" baking pan. Layer half of eggplant slices in pan; cover with all of sausage mixture. Layer remaining eggplant slices on top. Top with remaining pasta sauce; sprinkle with shredded cheese. Cover with aluminum foil. Bake at 350 degrees for 30 minutes, or until bubbly and cheese is melted. Makes 4 to 6 servings.

Over dinner, ask your children to tell you about books they're reading at school and return the favor by sharing books you loved as a child. You may find you have some favorites in common!

Autumn in a Bowl

Narita Roady
Pryor, OK

When my girls were younger, we couldn't always afford stew meat. (Still can't...LOL!) So I decided to make a stew with ground beef and it needed to be a recipe that didn't have to cook all day. Gradually through the years, this recipe evolved. It's warm, delicious and hits the spot on a cold day! Wonderful with hot buttered cornbread. It also freezes well. I make extra to freeze for busy days!

1 to 2 T. oil
1 lb. lean ground beef
1/2 onion, chopped
2 to 3 stalks celery, chopped
salt and pepper to taste
1-1/2 t. Italian seasoning
14-1/2 oz. can diced tomatoes
8-oz. can tomato sauce
2 to 3 potatoes, peeled and diced
1-1/4 c. frozen mixed vegetables
2 t. beef soup base, or 2 cubes
   beef bouillon

Spray a Dutch oven with non-stick vegetable spray; add oil and heat over medium heat. Add beef, onion, celery, salt and pepper; cook until nearly browned. Drain; stir in Italian seasoning. Add tomatoes with juice, tomato sauce, potatoes and frozen vegetables; stir to mix. (If desired to save time, steam or sauté potatoes and vegetables in a separate pan while beef is browning.) Add enough water to fill pan 3/4 full. Bring to a low boil; simmer for 5 minutes. Stir in soup base or bouillon cubes. Cover and simmer until vegetables are tender, stirring occasionally. Makes 8 servings.

Hosting dinner on Thanksgiving? Ask everyone to bring a baby photo. Have a contest...the first person to guess who's who gets a prize!

Family-Favorite
Comfort Foods

Slow-Cooker Sesame Ribs

Paula Marchesi
Auburn, PA

I love making different recipes for my family. This one is so good, I made it a permanent staple at our house.

1 onion, halved and sliced
3/4 c. brown sugar, packed
1/2 c. catsup
1/4 c. soy sauce
1/4 c. honey
2 T. vinegar

3 cloves garlic, minced
1 t. ground ginger
5 lbs. boneless country-style
   pork ribs
2 T. green onions, chopped
2 T. toasted sesame seed

Place onion slices in the bottom of a 6-quart slow cooker; set aside. In a large bowl, stir together brown sugar, catsup, soy sauce, honey, vinegar, garlic and ginger. Add ribs and turn to coat well. Arrange ribs over onion in slow cooker; spoon sauce over ribs. Cover and cook on low setting for for 5 to 7 hours, until ribs are very tender. At serving time, place ribs on a serving platter. Sprinkle with green onions and sesame seed; serve sauce from slow cooker on the side. Makes 6 servings.

Alongside saucy ribs or fried chicken, set out all the fixin's for a baked potato bar at dinner...let everyone choose their favorite toppers. A fun way to serve a satisfying, simple meal.

Laura Ann's Chicken Pot Pie

Lisa Ann Panzino DiNunzio
Vineland, NJ

This pot pie is delicious and easy to make...it is one of my sister Laura's most-requested recipes! The recipe makes two pot pies that will be very rustic in appearance.

2 T. extra-virgin olive oil
1 T. butter
3 to 4 carrots, peeled and sliced
3 to 4 stalks celery, sliced
1 c. onion, chopped
1 t. dried thyme
salt and pepper to taste

1/4 c. all-purpose flour
3 c. low-sodium chicken broth
1/4 c. whipping cream
1-1/2 c. frozen peas
3 c. cooked chicken, shredded
4 9-inch pie crusts, unbaked

In a saucepan over medium heat, combine oil, butter, carrots, celery, onion and seasonings. Cook until vegetables are fork-tender. Sprinkle flour over vegetable mixture while stirring; cook for one minute. Increase heat to medium-high. Add chicken broth and cook until mixture thickens, stirring occasionally. Add cream, peas and chicken. Reduce heat to medium-low; simmer for 3 to 4 minutes. Arrange 2 pie crusts in 9" pie plates; divide filling between crusts. Top each pie with another additional crust. Using a fork, crimp the edges of crust together. Make a few slits in center of crusts with a knife tip, to allow steam to escape. Set pot pies on a large baking sheet. Bake at 400 degrees for 45 to 55 minutes, until filling is bubbly and crust is golden. Allow pies to cool slightly; cut into wedges and serve. Makes 2 pies; each serves 4 to 6.

Using frozen crusts for a 2-crust pie? Remove one crust from its disposable pie plate and set it upside-down on wax paper to thaw while preparing your pie. When it's time to add the top crust, it will be thawed and pliable.

Family-Favorite
Comfort Foods

Chicken Poppy Seed

Nicole Westman
Painesville, OH

This is one of my favorite meals that my mother made for us kids when we were growing up! I love to serve it over steamed rice, with a green salad or vegetable on the side. Yummy!

3 boneless, skinless chicken
   breasts
garlic powder, dried parsley,
   salt and pepper to taste
10-3/4 oz. can cream of
   chicken soup

1 c. sour cream
1 t. poppy seed
1/4 to 1/2 c. butter, melted
1 to 2 sleeves buttery round
   crackers, crushed
cooked rice or noodles

In a large saucepan, cover chicken with water; bring to a boil. Simmer over medium heat until chicken is cooked through, 20 to 30 minutes; drain. Dice chicken; add seasonings as desired. In a bowl, mix with chicken soup, sour cream and poppy seed. Spread in a greased 13"x9" baking pan. Combine melted butter and crushed crackers; spread over chicken mixture. Bake, covered, at 350 degrees for 45 minutes to one hour, until hot and bubbly. Serve over cooked rice or noodles. Makes 5 to 6 servings.

Harvest Pork Chops

Stacey Loomis
Goode, VA

I love using my sister's homemade maple syrup, homegrown sweet potatoes and freshly picked peaches for this recipe!

4 pork chops
1 T. lime juice
1/4 t. ground ginger
3 sweet potatoes, peeled
   and cubed

3 peaches, pitted and sliced
1/4 c. pure maple syrup
Optional: 1 T. cinnamon-sugar,
   1 T. crushed pecans

Arrange pork chops in a 13"x9" baking pan coated with non-stick vegetable spray. Drizzle pork chops with lime juice; sprinkle with ginger. Layer sweet potatoes and peaches over pork chops; drizzle with maple syrup. If desired, sprinkle with cinnamon-sugar and pecans. Cover with aluminum foil. Bake at 400 degrees for 35 minutes, or until pork chops are cooked through and sweet potatoes are tender. Serves 4.

Grandy's Chicken Tetrazzini

Sheila Craig Peregrin
Lancaster, PA

Grandy was a wonderful cook. This recipe makes two big pans, travels well and is so delicious! It had a way of being the most-requested dish at grandchildren's high-school musical cast parties, bridal and baby showers and covered-dish gatherings. It is a creamy, cheesy comfort food dinner on a cold night, and leftovers (if there are any!) can be frozen and reheated for future meals. It is great accompanied by a tossed green salad, three-bean salad or coleslaw. Use leftover cooked turkey if you like.

3 lbs. boneless, skinless
   chicken breasts
seasoned salt and pepper to taste
1 T. butter
1 T. olive oil
1 lb. sliced mushrooms
1 c. onion, diced
1 T. garlic, minced
24-oz. pkg. spaghetti, broken
   into thirds and uncooked

24-oz. can cream of mushroom
   soup
2 c. plus 6 T. grated Parmesan
   cheese, divided
2 c. whipping cream
1 c. 2% milk
1/4 c. dry bread crumbs, divided
1/4 c. butter, diced and divided

Arrange chicken pieces in a greased 13"x9" baking pan; sprinkle with seasoned salt and pepper. Cover and bake at 350 degrees for about one hour, until cooked through. Cool slightly; cut chicken into bite-size pieces. Set aside, or refrigerate until needed. Melt butter with oil in a skillet over low heat; add mushrooms. Cook for about 10 minutes, until almost done. Add onion and garlic; cook until onion is translucent. Set aside, or transfer to a container and refrigerate until needed. When ready to bake, cook spaghetti according to package directions; drain. Meanwhile, in a very large bowl, whisk together mushroom soup, 2 cups Parmesan cheese, cream and milk. Add chicken and mushroom mixture; stir well. Add cooked spaghetti; stir until well combined. Divide into 2 greased 13"x9" baking pans. Divide bread crumbs between pans; dot evenly with butter and sprinkle with remaining Parmesan cheese. Bake, uncovered, at 350 degrees for about 45 minutes, until bubbly and lightly golden. Makes 2 pans; each serves 8.

Family-Favorite
Comfort Foods

Kielbasa Bake

Maureen Charnigo
Medina, OH

This recipe was given to me 25 years ago by my husband's Aunt Joan, may she rest in peace. I have made it well over a hundred times, for every bridal shower, baby shower and family function, from birthday parties to graduations. It's so easy and delicious. I usually serve it over steamed rice.

3 lbs. Kielbasa or other smoked
    sausage, sliced
3/4 c. brown sugar, packed

12-oz. bottle chili sauce
15-1/4 oz. can crushed pineapple

Combine all ingredients in a roaster pan; do not drain pineapple. Bake, uncovered, at 350 degrees for one to 1-1/2 hours. May also combine all ingredients in a 4-quart slow cooker; cover and cook on low setting for 3 to 4 hours. Makes 6 to 8 servings.

Loaded Pierogi Skillet

Krista Marshall
Fort Wayne, IN

We love pierogi and the frozen ones are so easy to work with. This quick-cooking dish can be on the table in about 20 minutes and is perfect with chicken, pork and beef. Or double the recipe for a main dish and add a tossed salad on the side. Yum!

2 to 3 T. butter
16-oz. pkg. frozen cheese
    pierogi, uncooked
2-1/2 oz. pkg. real bacon bits

1 c. shredded sharp Cheddar
    cheese
2 green onions, chopped

Melt butter in a large skillet over medium high heat; add pierogi. Sauté for 3 to 4 minutes per side, until golden. Sprinkle with bacon bits, cheese and onions. Reduce heat to low. Cover and cook for 5 minutes, or until cheese begins to melt. Serve immediately. Makes 4 servings.

Mom's Lasagna

Helen McKay
Edmond, OK

I remember my mom making this for dinner or company when I was in high school, some 50 years ago. It was a special dinner whenever she made this, served with homemade garlic bread and a crisp tossed salad. So good!

8-oz. pkg. lasagna noodles,
   uncooked
2 T. olive oil
3/4 c. onion, chopped
2 cloves garlic, minced
1 lb. ground beef
1 T. dried parsley
1-1/2 t. dried oregano
1/2 t. dried rosemary or basil

2-1/2 t. salt
1/4 t. pepper
2 c. tomato paste
2 c. hot water
16-oz. container cottage cheese
2 eggs, beaten
16-oz. pkg. shredded mozzarella
   cheese, divided
1/4 c. grated Parmesan cheese

Cook noodles according to package directions; drain. Meanwhile, heat oil in a skillet. Add onion and garlic; cook until soft. Add beef and seasonings; cook until browned and crumbly. Drain; stir in tomato paste and hot water. Simmer for 5 minutes and set aside. In a bowl, blend cottage cheese with beaten eggs. Spread a thin layer of beef sauce in the bottom of a greased 13"x9" baking pan. Layer with half of noodles, all of cottage cheese mixture, half of mozzarella cheese and half of remaining beef sauce. Repeat layers; sprinkle with Parmesan cheese. Bake, uncovered, at 350 degrees for 30 minutes, or until hot and bubbly. Cool for 10 minutes. Serves 8.

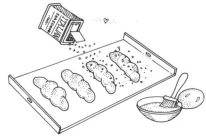

Bake some savory garlic twists for dinner. Separate refrigerated bread stick dough and lay flat on an ungreased baking sheet. Brush with olive oil; sprinkle with garlic salt and dried parsley. Give each bread stick a twist or two and bake as directed on the package.

Celebration
Appetizers

Taco Corn Dip

Stephanie Kemp
Lakeville, OH

I made this the first time for my husband and myself. Oh my,
it is delicious! I could eat it with a spoon, it is so good.
It's definitely a keeper in my book, and so easy!

2 7-oz. cans sweet corn &
    diced peppers, drained
10-oz. can original or hot diced
    tomatoes with green chiles,
    drained
8-oz. pkg. shredded Cheddar
    cheese

8 green onions, sliced
1 c. mayonnaise
1 c. sour cream
1 bunch fresh cilantro, chopped
1-oz. pkg. taco seasoning mix
scoop-type corn chips or
    tortilla chips

In a large bowl, combine all ingredients except chips; mix together.
Cover and refrigerate for one hour, or until serving time. Serve with
corn or tortilla chips. Serves 8.

Dress up the table with flower-trimmed pumpkins. Use a pointed
awl or ice pick to make holes in small pumpkins, then trim
the stems of fresh chrysanthemums and insert into holes.
Refrigerate pumpkins until party time to keep the mums fresh.

Celebration
Appetizers

Ellen's Thanksgiving Deviled Eggs

*Pat Martin
Riverside, CA*

*Our granddaughter Ellen requested deviled eggs as an appetizer for
Thanksgiving. Thinking about how I could shake things up a bit,
I came up with these two variations...they were gone in a flash!*

6 to 12 eggs, hard-boiled
    and peeled

salt and pepper to taste

Slice each hard-boiled egg in half lengthwise. Scoop egg yolks into a
bowl; mash well. Add variation #1 or #2 ingredients except garnish and
mix well; season with salt and pepper. Spoon mixture into egg whites;
garnish as desired. Cover and chill, or serve immediately. Makes one to
2 dozen.

Variation #1:

3 to 6 T. mayonnaise
3 to 6 T. sour cream
1 to 2 t. mustard

Garnish: 3 to 6 slices bacon,
    crisply cooked and crumbled

Variation #2:

3 to 6 T. mayonnaise
3 to 6 T. Dijon mustard
1 to 2 T. green onions,
    finely diced

1 to 2 t. picante sauce
Garnish: thin slices ripe avocado

Everyone loves deviled eggs! If there's no deviled egg plate handy,
simply line a serving plate with curly parsley or shredded
lettuce, then nestle the eggs in the greens.

Bread Pot Fondue

Karen Wilson
Defiance, OH

This delicious hot, cheesy appetizer makes a pretty presentation in its loaf.

1 round loaf Hawaiian bread
8-oz. pkg. shredded sharp
   Cheddar cheese
8-oz. pkg. cream cheese,
   softened
1-1/2 c. sour cream

1 c. cooked ham, diced
1/4 c. green onions, chopped
2 T. fresh chives, chopped
1 t. Worcestershire sauce
Optional: snack crackers

Hollow out bread loaf; reserve bread pieces and set aside. In a large bowl, combine cheeses and sour cream; mix until thoroughly blended. Stir in ham, onions, chives and Worcestershire sauce. Spoon dip into loaf. Wrap loaf with heavy-duty aluminum foil; set on a baking sheet. Bake at 350 degrees for 40 to 45 minutes, until dip is hot and bubbly. Serve with reserved chunks of bread and crackers, if desired. Makes 10 to 12 servings.

For an easy party spread guests will love, serve up a festive grazing board. On a large tray or platter, arrange a selection of smoked or cured deli meats, cheeses, crackers, nuts, fresh or dried fruits... even some gourmet mustard and preserves for dipping. Delicious!

Celebration
Appetizers

Cream Cheese Log with Dried Beef

Gladys Kielar
Whitehouse, OH

There's a cheese ball to enjoy for any gathering. Here is a good one that we love. Serve it on a plate, with a spreader alongside.

8-oz. container reduced-fat soft-style cream cheese, room temperature
1/2 c. reduced-fat mayonnaise
1 t. prepared horseradish, drained
1/2 c. shredded Swiss cheese

2-oz. pkg. dried beef, finely chopped
1 T. canned pimentos, drained and chopped
1/2 c. fresh chives or green onion tops, finely chopped
Melba toast slices

In a bowl, combine cream cheese, mayonnaise and horseradish. Beat with an electric mixer on medium speed until creamy. Stir in Swiss cheese, dried beef and pimentos. Form into a 8-inch log. Wrap log in plastic wrap; refrigerate for at least 2 hours. Spread chives or onion tops on wax paper. Unwrap cheese log and carefully roll in chives, coating completely. Rewrap in plastic wrap; refrigerate until serving time. Serve with Melba toast slices. Makes 8 servings.

If you love tailgating, but can't score tickets to the big stadium football game, round up your friends and tailgate at the local Friday-night high school game. Pack a picnic and cheer on your team!

Loaded Sweet Peppers

Vivian Marshall
Columbus, OH

*This is one of our favorite appetizers...sometimes it's our whole meal!
I love using one of each color of pepper, to keep it colorful. The peppers
stay crunchy and are soooo delicious! By using peppers instead of
nacho chips, these are also keto-friendly and low-carb.*

4 assorted sweet peppers, tops
   and seeds removed
1/2 lb. ground beef
1 T. garlic, minced
1 T. beef bouillon powder
1/2 c. white onion, finely
   chopped

2 jalapeño peppers, sliced and
   seeds discarded
1-1/2 c. shredded Mexican-blend
   cheese, divided
2 T. chopped black olives,
   drained
Garnish: salsa, sour cream

Cut each pepper into 4 wedges if small or 6 wedges if large. Arrange
close together on an aluminum foil-lined baking sheet coated with
non-stick vegetable spray; set aside. Brown beef in a skillet over
medium heat, adding garlic and bouillon; drain well. Top each pepper
wedge with a spoonful of onion, a spoonful of beef mixture and 2 slices
jalapeño pepper; sprinkle lightly with shredded cheese. Bake at
350 degrees for about 5 minutes, until cheese is melted. Remove
from oven; top with olives and remaining cheese. Return to oven for
10 minutes. Serve warm with salsa and sour cream. Serves 6 to 8.

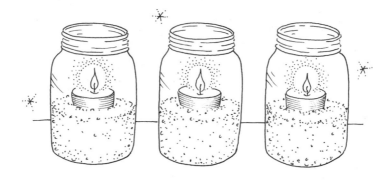

Need a quick table decoration? Fill Mason jars with coarse salt,
then tuck in a votive. The salt crystals will sparkle in the
flickering light...perfect for casual get-togethers.

Celebration
Appetizers

Slow-Cooker Hot Nacho Dip

*Pamela Myers
Auburn, IN*

My sister-in-law Laura is an outstanding cook and has shared many recipes with me. She shared this easy nacho dip years ago and it's a crowd favorite! It's a lot tastier than the usual dips made with ground beef. I make it whenever I'm asked to bring a snack.

16-oz. pkg. ground pork sausage
16-oz. pkg. hot ground pork
   sausage
16-oz. jar mild salsa
16-oz. jar medium salsa
16-oz. pkg. pasteurized process
   cheese, cubed

16-oz. pkg. Mexican-blend
   pasteurized process cheese,
   cubed
tortilla chips

In a large skillet over medium heat, brown all sausage. Drain; transfer to a 6-quart slow cooker. Layer with all salsa and all cheese. Cover and cook on low setting for about 3 hours, stirring occasionally. Serve with tortilla chips. Makes 20 to 25 servings.

Kim's Hot Corn Dip

*Bootsie Dominick
Suches, GA*

This is a great dip to serve while watching football, or anytime! The recipe came from my niece Kim. She has a lot of family & friends over for dinners and cook-outs, and always serves the best meals.

11-oz. can sweet corn & diced
   peppers, drained
1 c. shredded Monterey
   Jack cheese

1 c. mayonnaise
1 c. shredded Parmesan cheese
7 slices jalapeño pepper, chopped
scoop-type corn chips

In a lightly greased 2-quart casserole dish, combine all ingredients except chips. Bake at 350 degrees for about 25 minutes, until golden and heated through. Serve with corn chips. Makes 6 to 8 servings.

Welcome AUTUMN

Stuffed Mushrooms

Carmela Tallmeister
Ontario, Canada

Great appetizer! A perfect prelude to any
sit-down or buffet dinner.

20 button or cremini mushrooms
1/4 c. butter, melted
1/2 c. cream cheese, softened
1 T. fresh chives, chopped
1/4 t. garlic powder
1/8 t. salt

1/8 t. pepper
1/8 t. cayenne pepper
1/4 c. Italian-seasoned dry
   bread crumbs
1/4 c. grated Parmesan cheese

Remove mushroom stems; mince finely and set aside. Dip mushroom caps into melted butter until well coated; set aside. In another bowl, combine cream cheese, mushroom stems and seasonings; mix well. Stuff mushroom caps with mixture; arrange on an ungreased baking sheet. Combine bread crumbs and Parmesan cheese; sprinkle over mushroom caps. Bake at 350 degrees for 15 minutes, until bubbly. Cool; serve at room temperature. Makes about 1-1/2 dozen.

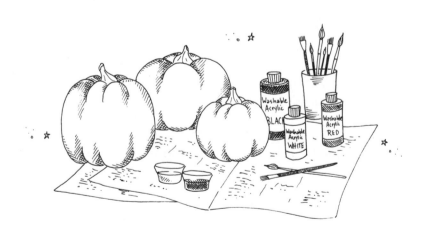

Host a pumpkin painting party. Provide acrylic paints, brushes and plenty of pumpkins...invite kids to bring their imagination and an old shirt to wear as a smock. Fun for all ages!

Celebration
Appetizers

Juju's Marinated Wings

*Patty Stevens
Springhill, LA*

Judy, also called Juju, was my cousin who was more like a sister to me. Sadly, she passed away at age 67 in November of 2019 of a rare form of dementia. This is her recipe for chicken wings. Men love them! They make great snacks to munch on while watching football games on television.

10 to 12 chicken wings,
    separated and wing
    tips discarded
8-oz. bottle soy sauce

16-oz. bottle Worcestershire
    sauce
1/2 c. smoke-flavored cooking
    sauce

Place chicken wings in a one-gallon plastic zipping bag; set aside. Mix all sauces in a bowl; pour over wings. Seal bag and turn to coat wings. Refrigerate for 12 to 24 hours, turning several times to marinate evenly. Transfer wings and marinade to a greased 15"x10" jelly-roll pan. Bake at 400 degrees for 60 minutes, turning occasionally, or until crisp and golden. Serves 4.

Mix up some homemade blue cheese dressing...yummy with wings!
Combine 3/4 cup softened cream cheese, 3/4 cup crumbled cheese
and 1/4 cup mayonnaise; blend well. For a colorful change, serve
with red pepper slices instead of celery sticks.

Welcome AUTUMN

Harvest Hash Party Mix

Tina Matie
Alma, GA

This recipe is super fun and yummy for get-togethers during the holiday season. I always make it to take it to our church's fall festival. Everybody loves this recipe, both young and old!

12-oz. pkg. bite-size crispy
    rice cereal squares
4 c. mini pretzel twists
7-oz. pkg. horn-shaped
    corn chips

1 c. candy corn
1 c. candy corn pumpkins
8-oz. pkg. candy-coated peanut
    butter candies

In a very large bowl, combine cereal, pretzels and chips; set aside while preparing Sauce. Pour sauce over cereal mixture; toss gently until evenly coated. Divide mixture between 2 large parchment paper-lined baking sheets; spread evenly. Bake at 275 degrees for 45 minutes, stirring every 15 minutes. Remove from oven and allow to cool. Transfer mixture to a large bowl; add candies and toss to combine. Store in an airtight container. Serves 12.

Sauce:

1 c. butter
1 c. light brown sugar, packed

2 T. vanilla extract

Melt butter in the microwave in a microwave-safe bowl. Add brown sugar and vanilla; whisk well until dissolved and combined.

A small house well filled is better than an empty palace.
–Thomas Chandler Haliburton

Celebration
Appetizers

Corn-Maize Popcorn

Arlene Smulski
Lyons, IL

*I made this fun treat one year for my Halloween get-together.
What a hit it was, for both adults and children!*

12 c. plain popped corn
1/2 c. pure maple syrup
1 T. butter

1 t. orange zest
1/2 t. salt
1 c. candy corn

Place popcorn in a large heat-proof bowl; remove any unpopped kernels and set aside. In a heavy saucepan, combine maple syrup, butter, orange zest and salt. Bring to a boil over medium-high heat, stirring often. Cook for 2 minutes without stirring. Pour mixture over popcorn; mix to coat completely. Spread coated popcorn in a single layer on a 17"x12" jelly-roll pan coated with non-stick vegetable spray. Bake at 300 degrees for 15 minutes; stir. Bake 3 minutes longer. Cool for 5 minutes; sprinkle candy corn evenly over popcorn and stir gently. Cool 25 minutes longer; store in an air-tight container. Makes about 13 cups.

Send everyone out on a harvest scavenger hunt...fun for the whole family. Make up a list of fall finds...a golden oak leaf, a red maple leaf, a pumpkin, a scarecrow, a red apple and a hay bale, just to name a few. It's not only lots of fun, it's a great way to get outside and enjoy the fabulous fall weather!

Chili Cheese Dog Chili

Tammy Kay Macias
Norfolk, VA

This is a recipe I put together for my local community chili cook-off. It was the year I won as "Mrs. Canyon Lake, California" and I wanted to create a fun and unique chili for the crowd to enjoy. It was a big hit!

8 beef hot dogs, cut into
   bite-size pieces
2 15-oz. cans favorite chili,
   or 3 c. homemade chili
28-oz. can crushed tomatoes
1/2 c. catsup
1/4 c. dill pickle relish
1/4 c. mustard

1 T. chili powder
salt and pepper to taste
8 hot dog buns, split
8-oz. pkg. shredded sharp
   Cheddar cheese
1 red onion, sliced
Optional: 1/4 c. jalapeño peppers,
   chopped

Coat a large skillet with non-stick vegetable spray. Add hot dogs; cook until browned on both sides. Transfer hot dogs to a 5-quart slow cooker. Add remaining ingredients except buns, cheese and onion. (Jalapeño may be added now, or reserved for topping.) Cover and cook on medium or low setting for 2 to 3 hours, until hot and bubbly. To serve, spoon chili into buns; garnish with cheese and onion. Or, spoon chili into bowls. Garnish with cheese and onion, and place buns on top. Serves 8 to 12.

Dress up chips & dip in a jiffy. Spoon dip into a tall wineglass and set it in the center of a large bowl. Arrange chips around it...all ready to serve!

Celebration
Appetizers

Fun Holiday Fruit Punch

Sandy Coffey
Cincinnati, OH

Something a little more fun for a holiday beverage! Kids and adults love it. I like to serve it with ice cubes made of frozen fruit juice or punch.

12-oz. can frozen orange juice concentrate
12-oz. can frozen grape juice concentrate
12-oz. can frozen lemonade concentrate

2 48-oz. bottles red fruit punch
2 qts. ginger ale, chilled
1 qt. cola beverage, chilled
Optional: orange and lemon slices

Thaw frozen juices slightly; combine all juices in a large pitcher. Cover and chill. At serving time, pour juice mixture into a punch bowl. Carefully pour in ginger ale and cola. Float orange and lemon slices on top, if desired. Makes about 6 quarts.

For a fruit-studded ice ring that won't dilute your party punch, arrange sliced oranges, lemons and limes in a ring mold. Pour in a small amount of punch and freeze until set. Add enough punch to fill mold and freeze until solid. To turn out, dip mold carefully in warm water.

Hot Dallas Dip

Nan Calcagno
Grosse Tete, LA

A perfect warm dip for family gatherings or any holiday. Serve with Melba toast, corn chips or crackers. Sooo good!

1 lb. ground beef
1 lb. ground pork sausage
1 onion, chopped
4 cloves garlic, chopped
32-oz. pkg. pasteurized process
    cheese, cubed

2 10-3/4 oz. cans cream of
    mushroom soup
15-1/4 oz. can diced tomatoes
    with green chiles, drained
    and chopped
4-oz. can diced green chiles

In a large deep skillet, combine beef and sausage with onion and garlic. Cook until browned and bubbly; drain. Add remaining ingredients. Cook and stir over low heat until cheese is melted. Simmer for a few more minutes, stirring constantly. Keep hot in a chafing dish or a small slow cooker set on low. Serves 20.

Honey-Mustard Dipping Sauce

Donna Wilson
Maryville, TN

This is a great blend of savory and sweet. I like to serve this delicious dip with homemade pretzels or hot chicken wings for any holiday events. So good!

1/2 c. mayonnaise
2 T. yellow mustard
1 T. Dijon mustard

2 T. honey
1-1/2 t. lemon juice

Combine all ingredients in a bowl; mix thoroughly. Cover and chill until serving time. Serves 8.

Set out a wooden bowl of walnuts so everyone can help themselves...don't forget the nutcracker!

Celebration
Appetizers

Rachel's Black Forest Cheese Ball *Rachel Williams*
Bokeelia, FL

This recipe was created for my daughter, who loves cheese balls.

8-oz. pkg. cream cheese,
   softened
3 to 6 thin slices deli Black Forest
   baked ham, chopped
1 T. mayonnaise-style salad
   dressing

1 T. Worcestershire sauce
1/8 t. garlic salt
1 t. onion, minced
1 c. shredded sharp
   Cheddar cheese
snack crackers

In a large bowl, combine all ingredients except shredded cheese and crackers. Mix well and set aside. Sprinkle shredded cheese on a piece of wax paper. Scoop cheese mixture onto the center of shredded cheese and shape into a ball. Add more shredded cheese on top, if desired. Cover and refrigerate at least one hour, or make a day ahead. Serve with crackers. Makes 8 servings.

Keep tailgating food cold...fill plastic bottles with homemade lemonade or iced tea, freeze and tuck into your picnic cooler. They'll thaw by mealtime.

Welcome AUTUMN

Pulled Pork Pastry Puffs

Michelle Newlin
Portage, PA

Great for a party appetizer!

3/4 lb. pulled pork
3/4 c. favorite barbecue sauce
17.3-oz. pkg. frozen puff pastry,
   thawed

1-1/4 c. shredded Cheddar
   cheese
1 egg, beaten
1 T. water

Combine pork and barbecue sauce in a bowl; toss to coat and set aside. Unfold thawed pastry sheets on a lightly floured surface. Cut each sheet into 9 squares, creating a total of 18 squares. Spoon a heaping tablespoonful of pork mixture and cheese down the center of each pastry square, corner to corner. Bring together 2 opposite corners of each square over pork. Press edges to seal, or fasten with a wooden toothpick. Arrange on a parchment paper-lined baking sheet. Whisk together egg and water; brush over puffs. Bake at 400 degrees for 15 to 18 minutes, until golden. Serve warm or at room temperature. Makes 2 dozen.

Nacho Popcorn

Liz Plotnick-Snay
Gooseberry Patch

I needed a party snack in a hurry and found everything for this recipe in my kitchen. It was a hit!

10 c. popped popcorn
1/4 c. butter, melted
1/4 c. grated Parmesan cheese

1 t. paprika
1/2 t. ground cumin
Optional: salt to taste

Place popcorn in a large bowl; remove any unpopped kernels. Drizzle with melted butter; toss to mix. Combine cheese and seasonings in a cup; sprinkle over popcorn. Season with salt, if desired. Toss to coat well and serve. Makes 10 cups.

Celebration
Appetizers

Chicken-Fried Bacon

Vickie
Gooseberry Patch

Just when you think bacon can't get any better! I like to serve this at tailgating parties, with ranch dressing for dipping. It's equally welcome at brunch, with white gravy on the side. Be sure to use corn flour, not cornmeal or cornstarch.

1 c. all-purpose flour
1 c. corn flour
1 T. salt
1 T. pepper

12-oz. can evaporated milk
1 lb. thick-sliced bacon
canola oil for frying

In a large shallow bowl, combine flours, salt and pepper. Pour evaporated milk into a separate dish. Coat each bacon slice with flour mixture; dip into milk and coat with more flour. Add 1/2 inch oil to a large heavy skillet; heat over medium-high heat to 375 degrees. Working in batches, add bacon slices to hot oil and cook until crisp and golden. Remove with a slotted spoon; drain on paper towels and cool. Makes one dozen.

Make a pumpkin cornucopia. Place a pumpkin on its flattest side, then hollow out the rounded side. Fill the opening with apples, leaves, bittersweet and rose hips. So simple, yet so pretty!

Welcome
AUTUMN

Tailgate Twisters

Tamara Long
Huntsville, AR

This recipe is great for parties, potlucks, or just snacking at home. It's good as an added side on taco night, too!

8-oz. pkg. cream cheese, softened
1 c. sour cream, excess liquid drained
1 to 2 c. shredded sharp Cheddar cheese
1-oz. pkg. taco seasoning mix
1/2 t. salt
1/4 t. pepper

14-oz. can chopped black olives, drained
4-oz. can diced green chiles, drained
Optional: 2-1/2 oz. pkg. real bacon pieces
4 10-inch flour tortillas
Optional: favorite salsa

In a large bowl, beat cream cheese until fluffy. Add remaining ingredients except tortillas and garnish; stir until well blended. Spread mixture on tortillas; roll up. Wrap in plastic wrap and refrigerate for 2 hours, or overnight. Slice into rounds, 1/2-inch thick. Arrange on a serving plate; serve chilled with salsa. Makes 12 servings.

Invite friends to spend an evening around the fire pit. A simple meal of roasted hot dogs and baked beans is perfect. As the fire burns down, it's time to tell ghost stories (not too scary, if little kids are present) and admire the stars in the clear night sky. Ahhh...autumn!

Celebration
Appetizers

Sweet & Spicy Jalapeños

Caroline Britt
Cleveland, TX

*This is a traditional recipe with my little spin on the grill...
perfect for outdoor entertaining. Delicious!*

8-oz. pkg. cream cheese,
   softened
1 c. shredded Cheddar cheese
18 jalapeño peppers, halved
   lengthwise and seeds
   removed

2 c. brown sugar, packed
2 lbs. maple-flavored bacon
1/2 c. maple syrup

Blend cheeses in a bowl. Spoon mixture into jalapeño pepper halves. Place brown sugar in a shallow dish. Dip each bacon slice into brown sugar; wrap around a pepper half and secure with a wooden toothpick. Arrange on a preheated grill, using a grilling tray if possible. Grill, basting often with maple syrup, until bacon is crisp and golden. Makes about 3 dozen.

Lengths of burlap are so easy to turn into a table runner...
simply cut and fringe the edges! Wonderful for
harvest-time gatherings.

Welcome AUTUMN

Spinach-Artichoke Bites

Karen Wilson
Defiance, OH

I can never resist a dish that includes spinach and artichokes! This is one of my favorites.

8-oz. tube refrigerated
   crescent rolls
1-1/2 c. mayonnaise
1-1/2 c. shredded Parmesan
   cheese
1 T. Dijon mustard
1 t. lemon juice

1 T. Worcestershire sauce
1/2 t. garlic powder
1 c. frozen chopped spinach,
   thawed and well drained
2 14-oz. cans artichoke quarters,
   drained and chopped

Unroll dough on a greased 13"x9" baking sheet. Press to cover pan and press together perforations. In a bowl, combine remaining ingredients. Stir carefully to blend. Spread mixture over dough. Bake at 350 degrees for 15 to 20 minutes, until bubbly and crust is golden. Cut into squares and serve warm. Makes 16 pieces.

For a Halloween party, offer a selection of creepy foods and beverages...label with table tents in your spookiest handwriting. Have a specialty that isn't Halloween-ish? Just give it a spooky new name!

174

Celebration
Appetizers

Mini Cheese Balls on a Stick

LaDeana Cooper
Batavia, OH

Who doesn't love a delicious cheese ball? This one-bite party treat is great for a one-hand carry for those on the move.

2 8-oz. pkgs. cream cheese, softened
2-1/2 oz. jar dried beef, finely diced
1 bunch green onions, finely diced
1/4 to 1/2 t. Worcestershire sauce
pretzel sticks

In a large bowl, beat cream cheese with an electric mixer on medium speed until smooth. Add beef, onion and Worcestershire sauce; mix until well combined. Line a melon baller with a piece of plastic wrap. Scoop out mixture and turn out on platter. Cover and refrigerate until set set. Just before serving, insert a pretzel stick in each ball. Serves 10 to 12.

Variations:

• Roll balls in finely shredded sharp Cheddar cheese.

• Dip bottoms of balls in nacho tortilla or "pigskin" dust. Add chips or pork rinds to a food processor and whirl into "dust."

Lemon Cider

Lynda Hart
Bluffdale, UT

This is a warm addition to a fall game night gathering...equally refreshing served over ice for supper on the lawn.

1 gal. apple cider
12-oz. can frozen lemonade concentrate, thawed
Garnish: 2 cinnamon sticks, or 1 lemon, thinly sliced

To serve warm, combine cider, lemonade concentrate and cinnamon sticks in a soup pot. Heat until hot. To serve cold, chill cider; pour into a punch bowl or glass drink dispenser. Add concentrate and stir. Garnish with lemon slices. Makes 4-1/2 quarts.

Welcome AUTUMN

Autumn Apple Cheese Ball

Judy Phelan
Macomb, IL

A yummy treat that doesn't take long to fix! We prefer to roll the cheese ball in cashews...our favorite nut.

3/4 c. cashews or walnut halves
8-oz. pkg. cream cheese, room
   temperature
1-1/2 c. shredded sharp
   Cheddar cheese
1/2 green apple, cored and diced

1 T. caramel topping
1/8 t. nutmeg
assorted crackers
Garnish: additional caramel
   topping

Toast nuts in a skillet over medium-high heat, stirring often, until beginning to brown. Remove from heat and cool; chop into small pieces. Stir together cheeses in a large bowl. Add apple, caramel topping and nutmeg; mix well. Use your hands to roll into a ball. Spread nuts on a plate; roll cheese ball to coat well. Drizzle with extra caramel topping and serve with crackers. Serves 12.

Cranberry Chicken Spread

Charlotte Smith
Tyrone, PA

I always make this spread when entertaining. It's a great hit! I serve with assorted crackers, or even on mini kaiser rolls. Once you start, you'll want another bite, then another, then another!

1-3/4 c. cooked chicken,
   finely chopped
1 c. walnuts, finely chopped
2/3 c. plus 2 T. mayonnaise
1 stalk celery, finely chopped

1/2 c. onion, finely chopped
1/2 c. sweetened dried
   cranberries, chopped
1/2 to 1 t. salt
assorted crackers

In a large bowl, combine all ingredients except crackers; mix well. Cover and chill 3 to 4 hours to allow flavors to blend. Serve with crackers. Makes about 4 cups.

Celebration
Appetizers

Caramel Cream Cheese Dip

Georgia Muth
Penn Valley, CA

I've served this easy, quick dip at parties and family get-togethers.
It's scrumptious with sliced apples.

8-oz. pkg. cream cheese,
   softened
1/4 c. powdered sugar
1/4 t. vanilla extract

12-1/4 oz. jar caramel topping
8-oz. pkg. toffee baking bits
sliced Fuji or Gala apples

Combine cream cheese, powdered sugar and vanilla in a large bowl.
Beat with an electric mixer on medium speed until well blended. Spread
in a 9" pie plate. Spoon caramel topping over cream cheese; sprinkle
with toffee bits. Serve with sliced apples. Serves 10 to 12.

Jacki's Pumpkin Dip

Jacki Smith
Fayetteville, NC

My family & friends love this dip at all fall events. I always make
a double batch and send them home with a bowl of dip,
along with some gingersnaps for dipping!

15-oz. can pumpkin
8-oz. pkg. cream cheese,
   softened
7-oz. jar marshmallow creme

1/2 c. powdered sugar
2 t. pumpkin pie spice
gingersnap cookies

In a large bowl, combine all ingredients except gingersnaps. Beat with
an electric mixer on medium speed until well blended. Cover and chill;
serve with gingersnaps. Serves 6 to 8.

A hollowed-out pumpkin or squash is a fun way
to serve favorite dips.

Phyllis's Shrimp Dip

Courtney Stultz
Weir, KS

My husband and I started dating in high school. For every family gathering I've been around for, his step-mom would make this shrimp dip recipe that came from her friend Phyllis. It is by far his favorite appetizer. I made a couple of changes and we still enjoy it today... although I think he'll always prefer it made by his step-mom!

8-oz. pkg. cream cheese,
  softened
1/2 c. sour cream
4 green onions, finely chopped
1/2 t. garlic powder

1/2 t. pepper
6-oz. can tiny shrimp, drained
1 c. shredded Cheddar cheese
sliced vegetables, crackers

In a serving bowl, combine cream cheese, sour cream, onions, garlic powder and pepper. Stir until well combined. Fold in shrimp and shredded cheese. Cover and chill until serving time. Serve with sliced vegetables or crackers. Makes 10 servings.

Make a batch of warm crostini to serve with dips and spreads.
Thinly slice a loaf of French bread. Melt together 1/2 cup butter
with 1/2 cup olive oil and brush over one side of each slice.
Place on a baking sheet and bake at 300 degrees for
a few minutes, just until crisp and toasty.

Celebration
Appetizers

Cream Cheese Tuna Spread

Teresa Verell
Roanoke, VA

This tasty recipe is a family favorite. It is always requested for picnics and potluck dinners.

8-oz. pkg. cream cheese, softened
6-oz. can albacore tuna, drained and flaked
1 c. sweet onion, chopped
1/2 c. mayonnaise
1/2 c. chopped walnuts
1 T. lemon juice
buttery round crackers

In a large bowl, combine all ingredients except crackers; mix well. Cover and chill until serving time. Spread on crackers. Serves 5.

Ham & Cheese Pinwheels

Marian Forck
Chamois, MO

I got this recipe from my daughter's mother-in-law Tess. We like sharing our recipes and I love when she makes such good food. She is a really good cook!

8-oz. container whipped cream cheese
1 T. ranch salad dressing mix
1 clove garlic, minced
9 thin slices deli baked ham

Combine cream cheese, dressing mix and garlic in a bowl; blend well. Spread over each ham slice, roll up tightly. Cover and refrigerate for 2 hours. Cut into one-inch slices; arrange on a plate. Serves 8.

Gather pine cones and brush lightly with craft glue, then sprinkle with clear glitter...sparkly heaped in a wooden bowl!

Marlene's Muffaletta Pinwheels

Marlene Lenio
Cortland, OH

On my first trip to New Orleans, I discovered beignet doughnuts and muffaletta sandwiches, and loved both. I decided to try my hand at creating pinwheels using ready-made muffaletta mix...they were a hit at the last Super Bowl party! This recipe can be made a day ahead.

16-oz. jar muffaletta mix
  olive salad
Optional: 2-1/4 oz. can black
  olives, drained and diced
4 12-inch sandwich wraps or
  flour tortillas, any flavor

2 8-oz. pkgs. cream cheese,
  softened
Optional: favorite shredded
  cheese
8-oz. pkg. sliced pepperoni

Drain muffaletta mix through a fine strainer; transfer to a bowl. Add olives, if using; mix well and set aside. Spread each sandwich wrap or tortilla with cream cheese; sprinkle with shredded cheese, if desired. Spread 1/4 of muffaletta mixture over cream cheese and top with 1/4 of pepperoni slices. Roll up carefully, slightly pressing down pepperoni so it does not slide out. Wrap each roll in plastic wrap, twisting ends tightly. Refrigerate rolls. At serving time, unwrap, slice into 1/2-inch slices and arrange on a serving tray. Makes about 4 dozen.

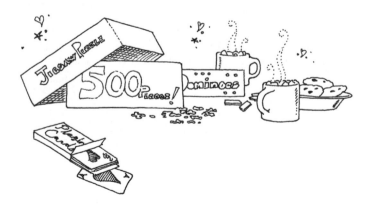

Set out a variety of games and puzzles when family & friends
are visiting. Pull out your childhood favorites...
sure to spark memories and laughter.

Celebration
Appetizers

Ham & Onion Tarts

Jeanine Watsko
Newtown, PA

These luscious tarts will be a hit at your next party or brunch.

2 T. butter
1 c. onion, thinly sliced
3-oz. pkg. sliced baked ham,
   coarsely chopped
1 sheet frozen puff pastry,
   thawed

2 eggs, beaten
1/2 c. sour cream
1/8 t. ground nutmeg
3 slices Swiss cheese, quartered
2 T. fresh chives, snipped

Melt butter in a large skillet over medium-low heat; add onion and ham. Cook for 12 to 14 minutes, stirring occasionally, until onion is tender and golden. Remove from heat. Meanwhile, unfold pastry; cut into 12 squares. Press each square into the bottom and up the sides of a lightly greased muffin cup; set aside. In a bowl, whisk together eggs, sour cream and nutmeg. Add onion mixture; mix well. Spoon into pastry cups; top with Swiss cheese and chives. Bake at 400 degrees for 12 to 14 minutes, until filling is set in the center and edges of pastry are golden. Transfer tarts to wire racks; cool slightly and serve. Makes one dozen.

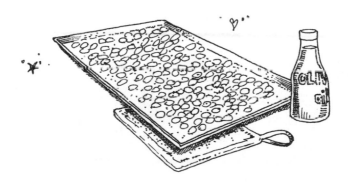

Toast pumpkin seeds for a tasty treat. Rinse seeds and pat dry. Toss with olive oil to coat, spread on a baking sheet and sprinkle with salt. Bake at 350 degrees for 10 to 15 minutes, until crisp and crunchy.

Welcome AUTUMN

Mom's Cranberry Sauerkraut Meatballs

Paula Marchesi
Auburn, PA

These are a must at potlucks, parties and Sunday football! Simple &
super easy to make...all made in one slow cooker, easy to transport.
For a change, use barbecue sauce instead of the chili sauce.

14-oz. can whole-berry cranberry
  sauce
12-oz. bottle chili sauce
14-oz. can sauerkraut, drained
  and rinsed

3/4 c. brown sugar, packed
32-oz. pkg. frozen cooked
  meatballs, thawed
Optional: chopped fresh parsley

In a 4-quart slow cooker, combine cranberry and chili sauces, sauerkraut
and brown sugar. Stir until mixed. Add meatballs; stir gently. Cover and
cook on low setting for 4 to 5 hours, until bubbly and heated through.
If desired, top with chopped parsley. Makes about 5 dozen.

For a quick & easy doorstep welcome, top decorative urns
with plump pumpkins. Orange pumpkins are oh-so cheerful,
or try white or green pumpkins for a change.

Celebration
Appetizers

Barbecued Hot Wings

Edward Kielar
Whitehouse, OH

*We serve these wings with blue cheese and celery sticks. Add
hot sauce and cayenne to suit your own heat level.*

8-oz. bottle Italian salad dressing
1/2 to 3/4 c. hot pepper sauce
1/8 to 1/2 t. cayenne pepper,
   to taste

12 chicken wings, separated
   and wing tips discarded
2 T. butter, melted

In a bowl, combine salad dressing, hot pepper sauce and cayenne
pepper. Reserve 1/2 cup for basting; cover and refrigerate. Add
remaining sauce to a large plastic zipping bag; add chicken wings.
Close bag and turn to coat wings. Refrigerate overnight, turning bag
occasionally. Drain, discarding marinade. Grill wings, covered, over
medium heat for 12 to 16 minutes, turning occasionally. Add butter to
reserved sauce; brush over wings. Grill, uncovered, for 8 to 10 minutes
longer, until chicken juices run clear, basting and turning several times.
Serves 8.

Real Good Cream Cheese Dip

R.E. Rohlof
Hickville, OH

Ready in a jiffy! Serve with your favorite chips.

8-oz. pkg cream cheese, softened
1 c. sour cream

3-oz. pkg dried beef, chopped
1 t. dried, minced onions

Combine all ingredients in a bowl; mix until thoroughly blended. Cover
and chill until serving time. Makes 8 servings.

Let guests know where the
party is! Fly a team banner
from the car antenna or porch.

Welcome AUTUMN

Spiced Maple Pecans

JoAnn
Gooseberry Patch

Yummy...perfect for party munching!

1 lb. pecan halves
1/2 c. pure maple syrup
1 T. ground cumin

1 t. cayenne pepper
1 t. kosher salt

Combine all ingredients in a large bowl; mix well. Spread in a single layer on a parchment paper-lined baking sheet. Bake at 350 degrees for 15 minutes; stir. Bake an additional 10 minutes. Cool for 5 minutes; stir to loosen individual pieces. Cool completely; store in an airtight container. Makes one pound.

Swedish Nuts

Lisa Ashton
Aston, PA

*This is a recipe that my mother handed down to me.
She loved making it for the holidays.*

3-1/2 c. walnut or pecan halves
2 egg whites, room temperature
1 c. sugar

1/8 t. salt
1/2 c. butter, melted

Spread nuts on an ungreased baking sheet. Bake at 325 degrees for about 10 minutes, stirring a few times, until toasted. Remove from oven; cool. In a large bowl, beat egg whites with an electric mixer on medium-high speed until soft peaks form. Slowly beat in sugar and salt in egg white mix. Add nuts; toss to coat well. Spread melted butter on same baking sheet; spread nuts on pan. Bake at 325 degrees for 20 to 25 minutes, stirring every few minutes. Remove from oven; let cool on baking sheet. Break up any clumps and serve. Makes 3-1/2 cups.

A fallen leaf is nothing more than a summer's wave goodbye.
–Unknown

Shareable
Desserts &
Cookies

Michigan Apple & Cherry Crisp

Nancy Lanning
Lancaster, SC

Growing up in Michigan, we had the best apples and cherries. I got this recipe at the Cherry Festival in Traverse City, Michigan, many years ago and have made it over and over. There isn't anything more delicious than a bowl of this warm apple & cherry crisp with ice cream on top!

4-1/2 c. assorted baking apples, peeled, cored and very thinly sliced
1 c. frozen tart cherries, thawed
1/2 c. brown sugar, packed
1/2 c. sugar
1/4 c. all-purpose flour
1 T. butter, melted
1 t. lime juice
1/2 t. almond extract
Garnish: ice cream or whipped cream

In a large bowl, combine all ingredients except garnish; mix well. Transfer to a buttered 10" pie plate or 9"x9" baking pan. Cover fruit mixture with Crumb Topping. Bake at 375 degrees for 30 minutes, or until bubbly and golden. Serve topped with ice cream or whipped cream. Makes 8 servings.

Crumb Topping:

1-1/2 c. all-purpose flour
1-1/2 c. sugar
1/4 t. salt
3/4 c. butter, softened

Combine all ingredients; mix until crumbly.

Warm homemade desserts are scrumptious topped with freshly whipped cream. For the fluffiest whipped cream possible, always make sure the bowl and beaters are chilled.

Fudge Jumbles

Carol Barnaby
Topeka, KS

One of my favorites from an old hometown cookbook. This recipe is a crowd-pleaser and is requested when my adult children come home for a visit. Depending on the occasion, I like to add a half-cup of flaked coconut or chopped pecans to the oat mixture.

1/2 c. plus 1 T. butter, softened
   and divided
1 c. brown sugar, packed
1 egg, beaten
1 t. vanilla extract
2 c. quick-cooking oats,
   uncooked

3/4 c. all-purpose flour
1 t. baking soda
1 c. semi-sweet chocolate chips
14-oz. can sweetened
   condensed milk

In a large bowl, blend together 1/2 cup butter, brown sugar, egg and vanilla. Add oats, flour and baking soda; stir to combine. Reserve one cup oat mixture for topping. Pat remaining mixture into the bottom of a greased 13"x9" baking pan; set aside. In a small saucepan, combine chocolate chips, condensed milk and remaining butter. Cook over low heat until melted and smooth, stirring often. Spoon over crust in pan. Crumble reserved oat mixture over chocolate layer. Bake at 350 degrees for 30 minutes, or until set and golden. Cool slightly and cut into bars. Makes 2 dozen.

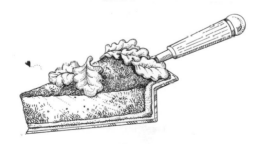

Over the river, and through the wood,
now Grandmother's cap I spy!
Hurrah for the fun! Is the pudding done?
Hurrah for the pumpkin pie!
–Lydia Maria Child

Glazed Cranberry-Almond Squares

Ellen Folkman
Crystal Beach, FL

A sweet-tart treat that's perfect for fall gatherings!
If using frozen cranberries, do not thaw them first.

1 c. butter, melted
2 c. all-purpose flour
2 c. sugar

3 eggs
1-1/2 t. almond extract
3 c. fresh or frozen cranberries

In a large bowl, with an electric mixer on medium speed, beat butter, flour and sugar until combined. Stir in eggs, one at a time, and extract. Fold in cranberries until most cranberries are covered in batter. Spray a 13"x9" baking pan with non-stick baking spray. Spread batter evenly in pan. Bake at 350 degrees for one hour. Cool bars completely; drizzle with Glaze. Cut into squares. Makes 12 to 15 squares.

Glaze:

1/4 c. powdered sugar
1/2 t. vanilla extract

2 t. water

Combine all ingredients; mix to a drizzling consistency.

Arrange homebaked goodies on a 3-tiered cake stand
for a delightful dessert tray that doesn't take up
much space on a buffet.

Shareable
Desserts & Cookies

Chocolate Marshmallow Cookies

Jessica Delia
Preble, NY

This is a family favorite that my grandmother, mother and aunts have been making for years. Even as adults, my girls still ask for these cookies! You can tint frosting to match the holidays as well.

1/2 c. shortening
1 c. sugar
1 egg, beaten
1/4 c. milk
1 t. vanilla extract
1-3/4 c. all-purpose flour

1/2 t. baking soda
1/2 c. baking cocoa
1/2 t. salt
18 marshmallows, halved
Garnish: favorite frosting

In a bowl, combine all ingredients except marshmallows and garnish; mix well. Scoop dough by tablespoonfuls onto ungreased baking sheets. Bake at 350 degrees for 8 minutes. Remove from oven; press 1/2 marshmallow onto each cookie, cut-side down. Return to oven and bake 2 minutes. Cool; spread with frosting. Makes 3 dozen.

Jam Cupboard Squares

Agnes Ward
Ontario, Canada

An easy little recipe to enjoy...lots of flavors of jam to try!

2/3 c. butter, softened
1/2 c. sugar
2 egg yolks, beaten
1 T. milk

1/2 t. vanilla extract
1/8 t. salt
1-1/2 c. all-purpose flour
1/2 c. favorite fruit jam

In a bowl, mix all ingredients except jam; pat into a greased or parchment paper-lined 9"x9" baking pan. Bake at 350 degrees for 20 minutes; cool slightly. Spread jam evenly over dough with the back of a spoon. Return to oven and bake another 20 minutes. Cool completely; cut into squares. Makes one dozen.

Fireside Applesauce Cake

*Betty Lou Wright
Fort Worth, TX*

When the air turns nippy, there's nothing like cozying up to the fireplace with a mug of warm cider and a piece of applesauce cake to welcome the new season. This so-easy, family-favorite recipe is especially delicious when topped with my dear mother-in-law's caramel frosting. It topped many a cake over the years, and I'm proud to continue the tradition. It's great on applesauce cake and even chocolate cake...my husband loves it by the spoonfuls!

15-1/4 oz. butter golden
   cake mix
1/3 c. yellow cake mix or
   all-purpose flour
3 eggs, beaten

1/4 c. water
2 c. applesauce
1/2 t. cinnamon
1/2 t. allspice
1/4 t. nutmeg

Combine all ingredients in a large bowl; stir to blend. Beat with an electric mixer on medium speed for 4 minutes. Pour batter into a 13"x9" baking pan coated with non-stick vegetable spray. Bake at 350 degrees for 40 to 45 minutes, until a toothpick tests clean. Cool. Pour Memaw's Caramel Frosting over cooled cake; cut into squares. Serves 12 to 16.

Memaw's Caramel Frosting:

1/2 c. butter
1/4 c. milk
1/4 t. salt

1 t. vanilla extract
2 c. powdered sugar, sifted
1 c. light brown sugar, packed

Melt butter in a saucepan over medium-low heat. Bring to a boil for 2 minutes, stirring constantly. Add milk; bring to a boil again. Cool to lukewarm. Stir in salt and vanilla; add sugars and mix well until dissolved.

Shareable
Desserts & Cookies

Indian Summer Candied Apples

Lynda Hart
Bluffdale, UT

One of my most memorable picnics was a fall leaf drive with Mom, Dad, my daughter, my niece and nephew. We went up the canyon and found a great spot with a picnic table along the river. Mom told the grandkids that she had a special surprise for them after they ate their lunch. She had made candied apples with tree twigs for handles. We all loved the surprise!

8 tree twigs or wooden
   treat sticks
8 small apples

4 c. sugar
1-3/4 c. water
1-1/2 c. chopped nuts

Insert a twig in each apple; set aside. Combine sugar and water in a large heavy saucepan over medium-high heat. Bring to a boil. Reduce heat to medium-low; simmer until mixture is golden. Don't use a spoon to stir the mixture, just swirl the pan occasionally so the sugar doesn't crystallize. Remove from heat; stir in nuts. Swirl each apple in the caramel to coat. Set on wax paper to cool and set. Wrap each apple in plastic wrap, leaving the twig exposed. Makes 8 apples.

Enjoy a spooky movie night at home on a chilly autumn evening.
Let the kids each invite a special friend and scatter plump cushions
on the floor for extra seating. Sure to be fun for everyone!

Welcome AUTUMN

Karen's Sunday Cheesecake

Karen Valenti
Kansas City, KS

When my kids were growing up, I used to bake this simple cheesecake often on Sundays. They loved it! It can be whipped up in just a few minutes and is delicious. Flavored with vanilla and almond extracts, it is lovely plain or garnished with fresh berries.

2 eggs, beaten
2 8-oz. pkgs. cream cheese,
   softened
1 c. sugar

1 t. vanilla extract
1 t. almond extract
Optional: fresh berries

Make Graham Cracker Crust; set aside. Combine eggs and cream cheese in a bowl; beat with an electric mixer on medium speed until smooth. Add sugar and extracts; beat until well blended. Pour into crust. Bake at 300 degrees for 45 to 50 minutes, until center is set with just a slight jiggle. Set pan on a wire rack; cool completely. Cover and chill for at least 4 hours before serving. Cut into wedges; top with fresh berries, if desired. Makes 8 servings.

Graham Cracker Crust:

3/4 c. graham cracker crumbs
1/2 c. sugar

1/4 c. butter, melted

Combine all ingredients; mix thoroughly. Transfer to a greased 9" round cake pan. Press evenly into the bottom and slightly up the sides to form a crust.

One of the secrets of a happy life
is continuous small treats.

–Iris Murdoch

Shareable
Desserts & Cookies

Grandma Teenie's Pumpkin Pie

Amy Mazza
Indianapolis, IN

*Everything Thanksgiving, my grandma's pumpkin pie was desired
more than the turkey itself. Each bite just melted in your mouth.
There were never any leftovers to take home!*

1-1/2 c. fresh pumpkin, cooked, or canned pumpkin	1 T. butter, softened
1 c. whole milk	1/4 t. salt
1 c. sugar	1/4 t. nutmeg
2 eggs, lightly beaten	1/4 t. cinnamon
	9-inch pie crust, unbaked

In a large bowl, combine all ingredients except pie crust. Mix
thoroughly; pour into pie crust. Bake at 425 degrees for 45 minutes,
or until a knife tip comes out clean. Cool completely; cut into wedges.
Makes 6 to 8 servings.

Cherry Crunch Bars

Susan Kruspe
Hall, NY

*I have been making this favorite dessert for many years. I sometimes
vary the fruit pie filling, or add twice the amount for extra fruit.
It is very good served warm à la mode!*

3/4 c. butter	1/2 t. baking soda
1 c. brown sugar, packed	1 t. salt
1-3/4 c. all-purpose flour	21-oz. can cherry pie filling
1-1/2 c. rolled oats, uncooked	

In a large bowl, blend together butter and brown sugar. Add flour,
oats, baking soda and salt; mix until crumbly. Press half of mixture
into a greased 13"x9" baking pan. Carefully spread pie filling over crust.
Sprinkle remaining crumb mixture over pie filling. Bake at 400 degrees
for 25 minutes, or until crumb topping is golden. Cool; cut into bars.
Makes one dozen.

Old-Fashioned Carrot Cake

Debbie McCullar
Checotah, OK

Our whole family loves this very moist and delicious cake with its scrumptious cooked icing. It's been in our family at least 40 years. Everyone always asks me to make it at Thanksgiving. It calls for a lot of butter and you can tweak that a little, but don't skimp too much or it'll end up being dry and not moist.

2-3/4 c. self-rising flour
2 c. sugar
1 T. cinnamon
2 c. carrots, peeled and grated

1-1/2 c. chopped pecans
1 c. oil
3 eggs, beaten
2 t. vanilla extract

In a bowl, sift together flour, sugar and cinnamon; set aside. In a large bowl, mix remaining ingredients. Slowly add flour mixture to carrot mixture; mix well. Pour batter into a greased and floured 13"x9" baking pan. Bake at 325 degrees for 25 to 35 minutes, until cake tests done. Cool cake completely; turn out of pan onto a serving platter. Poke holes in cake with a wooden spoon handle; pour Cooked Icing over cake. Cut into squares. Serves 20 to 24.

Cooked Icing:

1 c. evaporated milk
1 c. sugar
1 c. butter, sliced
3 egg yolks, beaten

1 t. vanilla extract
1 c. flaked coconut
1 c. chopped pecans

Combine all ingredients in a heavy saucepan. Cook over medium heat for 8 minutes, stirring often. Cool completely.

Dress up a frosted cake by adding a candy pumpkin to each piece...done in a snap!

Shareable
Desserts & Cookies

Stir & Drop Sugar Cookies

Joanne Wirth
Whiting, NJ

I've had this recipe since I was in grammar school. I make them for every holiday, and they go very quickly. Candy-coated chocolates or candy sprinkles can be placed on the cookies before baking...decorate them for any occasion!

2 eggs
2/3 c. oil
2 t. vanilla extract
3/4 c. sugar

2 c. all-purpose flour
2 t. baking powder
1 t. salt

Beat eggs in a large bowl. Stir in oil and vanilla; blend in sugar. Add flour, baking powder and salt; mix well. Drop dough by teaspoonfuls onto ungreased baking sheets. Bake at 375 degrees for 8 to 10 minutes. Cool on a wire rack. Makes about 3 dozen.

Carve an extra Jack-o'-Lantern and deliver it to elderly neighbors so they can enjoy some Halloween fun... what a sweet neighborly gesture!

Pumpkin-Filled Cannoli Cones

Sherri Tulini
Pitman, NJ

Such a fun treat! For the person who just can't get enough pumpkin,
or for a special take-along to holiday gatherings.

1/2 c. whipping cream
3/4 c. canned pumpkin
3/4 c. ricotta cheese
1/3 c. sugar
1/4 t. cinnamon
1/8 t. nutmeg

1/2 t. vanilla extract
8 sugar cones
2 T. mini semi-sweet chocolate
   chips
2 T. chopped walnuts
Optional: candy sprinkles

In a large bowl, beat cream with an electric mixer on high speed until
stiff peaks form; set aside. In another large bowl, combine pumpkin,
ricotta cheese, sugar, spices and vanilla. Beat on medium speed for
one minute. Carefully fold in whipped cream. Spoon or pipe mixture
into sugar cones. Top with chocolate chips, walnuts and sprinkles, if
desired. Chill until serving time. Makes 8 cones.

Visit the baking department at your neighborhood craft store
for mini candies and colorful sprinkles to dress up homemade
cookies and candies in a jiffy, all through the holidays.

Shareable
Desserts & Cookies

Milk Chocolate Pecan Fudge

Lisa Barger
Conroe, TX

This old-fashioned candy will have everyone asking for the recipe! It is very rich, so I cut mine into small squares.

7-oz. jar marshmallow creme
1-1/2 c. sugar
2/3 c. evaporated milk
1/4 c. butter
1/4 t. salt
3 c. milk chocolate chips
1 t. vanilla extract
1 c. chopped pecans

Line an 8"x8" baking pan with aluminum foil; set aside. In a large heavy saucepan, combine marshmallow creme, sugar, evaporated milk, butter and salt. Bring to a rolling boil over medium heat, stirring constantly. Boil for 5 minutes, stirring constantly. Remove from heat; stir in chocolate chips until melted and smooth. Add vanilla and pecans; mix until well blended. Pour fudge into prepared pan; smooth top of fudge. Cover and refrigerate for at least 3 hours, until firm. Turn fudge out onto a cutting board. Remove foil and cut into small squares. Makes 4 to 5 dozen.

Salted Nut Roll

Vickie Van Donselaar
Cedar, IA

You'll love this scrumptious candy...and it's so easy to make!

16-oz. jar salted dry-roasted
   peanuts, divided
12-oz. pkg. peanut butter chips
3 T. butter
14-oz. can sweetened
   condensed milk
10-oz. pkg. mini marshmallows

Spread half of peanuts in a greased 13"x9" baking pan; set aside. In a heavy saucepan over low heat, melt peanut butter chips with butter. Add condensed milk and marshmallows; cook and stir over low heat until blended. Spoon mixture over peanuts in pan; press down lightly. Top with remaining peanuts. Cover and refrigerate until cooled. Cut into bars. Makes 2 dozen.

Cranberry-White Chocolate Chip Cookies

Lisa Barger
Conroe, TX

This is a very delicious cookie that we love to eat anytime! You can replace the fresh cranberries with sweetened dried cranberries, but we love the fresh berries. I buy walnuts most of the time, because they are cheaper than pecans. But they both taste great!

1/2 c. butter
1/2 c. brown sugar, packed
1/2 c. sugar
3/4 t. baking soda
1/4 t. salt
1 egg, beaten

3/4 t. vanilla extract
1-1/2 c. all-purpose flour
1 c. fresh cranberries, chopped
1 c. white chocolate chips
3/4 c. chopped walnuts or pecans

In a large bowl, beat together butter and sugars until smooth. Add baking soda and salt; beat until well combined. Beat in egg and vanilla. Add flour and stir until combined. Using a wooden spoon, stir in cranberries, chocolate chips and nuts. Drop dough by rounded teaspoonfuls onto ungreased baking sheets, 2 inches apart. Bake at 375 degrees for 8 to 10 minutes, until edges are lightly golden. Remove cookies from baking sheet; cool on wire racks. Makes about 3 dozen.

Shelled or unshelled, nuts stay fresher longer if they're stored in the freezer...they're easier to crack when frozen, too.

Shareable
Desserts & Cookies

Salted Fudge Brownies

Kimberly Redeker
Savoy, IL

This is my one & only recipe for brownies. These don't take much more time than a box mix, but the results are out of this world! These brownies magically disappear every time I make them, no matter where I take them.

3/4 c. butter, divided
2-oz. sq. semi-sweet baking
   chocolate, chopped
1/4 c. plus 2 T. special dark
   baking cocoa

2 c. sugar
3 eggs, beaten
1-1/2 t. vanilla extract
1 c. all-purpose flour
1/2 t. sea salt

Linc a 9"x9" baking pan with aluminum foil; lightly coat foil with a a small amount of butter and set aside. In a saucepan over low heat, melt remaining butter with baking chocolate, stirring frequently. Remove from heat. Whisk in cocoa, sugar, eggs, vanilla and flour. Pour batter into pan; sprinkle with salt and swirl into batter. Bake at 350 degrees for about 35 minutes; center will still be a little soft. Set pan on a wire rack and allow to cool; cut into squares. Makes one dozen.

Make it easy on yourself when hosting a party. Instead of fussy decorated desserts, serve panfuls of easy treats like brownies and bar cookies. Guests are sure to be just as happy!

Crispy Rice Jack-o'-Lanterns

Debra Arch
Kewanee, IL

Years ago, I purchased one of these cute treats at a charity bake sale. My family loved the mix of crispy rice cereal and candy corn so much that every year at Halloween, we always made a double or triple batch to eat and to give out as special Halloween treats.

10-1/2 oz. pkg. mini
   marshmallows
1/4 c. butter
1/4 t. red food coloring

3/4 t. yellow food coloring
6 c. crispy rice cereal
Garnish: candy corn

In a microwave-safe bowl, melt marshmallows with butter on high for 2 minutes; stir. Microwave 2 more minutes, or until just melted. Remove from microwave. Add red and yellow coloring; mix very well. Add cereal and mix well. Using buttered hands, shape one heaping tablespoon of mixture into a round flat patty; place on wax paper. Press in 2 candy corn pieces with tips pointing up for eyes. Press in 3 candy corn pieces with tips pointing down for teeth. Press Pumpkin Stems onto the tops of pumpkins. Cool thoroughly before serving. Makes 15 to 20 pumpkins.

Pumpkin Stems:

1 c. mini marshmallows
1 T. butter

1-1/4 c. crispy rice cereal
1/4 t. green food coloring

Microwave marshmallows with butter as directed above; add green coloring and mix well. Add cereal and mix well; shape into one-inch squares.

Shareable
Desserts & Cookies

Ida's Platters

Sandy Perry
Fresno, CA

When the fall weather arrives, this is a great cookie to enjoy with a cup of hot cocoa or apple cider. My mom made these cookies for me as a small child. I was the only child, and therefore Mom would spoil me and make me homemade goodies. This is one that I have made for years for my children when they were little. They now make them for their own children...so many memories!

2 c. shortening
2 c. dark brown sugar, packed
2 c. sugar
2 c. rolled oats, uncooked
2 c. bran flake cereal

4 eggs, beaten
2 t. baking powder
2 t. baking soda
2 t. vanilla extract
4 c. all-purpose flour

Combine all ingredients into a large bowl; mix until well blended. Drop dough onto greased baking sheets by tablespoonfuls. Bake at 350 degrees for 15 minutes. Cool cookies on a wire rack for 10 minutes. Makes 6 dozen.

A big glass apothecary jar makes a terrific cookie jar. Personalize it by using a glass paint pen to add a message like "Grandma's Special Cookies" and hearts or swirls, just for fun.

Old-Fashioned Bread Pudding

Toni Patton
Hillview, IL

*My most-requested recipe! I often double this batch and bake it in a
13x9 baking pan. Make sure you set the pan inside a larger pan to
which you've added water. This prevents the bread pudding from
drying out while it's baking.*

2 eggs, lightly beaten	1/4 t. salt
2-1/4 c. milk	2 c. bread cubes
1 t. vanilla extract	1/2 c. brown sugar, packed
1/2 t. cinnamon	1/2 c. raisins

Combine eggs, milk, vanilla, cinnamon and salt in a large bowl. Stir in
bread cubes and mix well; stir in brown sugar and raisins. Transfer
mixture to a greased 8" round cake pan. Set pan in another, slightly
larger pan; carefully pour a small amount of water into larger pan. Bake
at 350 degrees for 45 minutes. Serve warm, topped with warm Sauce.
Makes 9 servings.

Sauce:

1/2 c. butter, softened	1 T. cornstarch
1 c. powdered sugar	1 t. vanilla extract
1 c. cold water	

Beat butter and sugar until fluffy; set aside. In a saucepan over medium
heat, stir water and cornstarch together; cook until thickened. Combine
with butter mixture; stir well. Stir in vanilla.

Bread pudding is a delicious way to
use up day-old bread. Try French
bread, raisin bread or even leftover
doughnuts for an extra-tasty dessert.

Norwegian Apple Pie

Jennifer Eck
Pleasantville, PA

My Aunt Edie gave me this recipe for a crustless pie. It's delicious! This recipe is good for fall or any time of year. It is super easy to fix...you can even mix it in the pie plate, if you like. It makes its own crust. I've made it for family get-togethers and friends' housewarmings, and everyone always loves it.

3/4 c. sugar
1/2 c. all-purpose flour
1 t. baking powder
1/4 t. salt
1/4 t. cinnamon

1 egg, beaten
1 t. vanilla extract
1/2 c. chopped pecans or walnuts
1 c. apples, peeled, cored
   and diced

In a large bowl, mix sugar, flour, baking powder, salt and cinnamon; set aside. In a separate bowl, stir together egg, vanilla, nuts and apples. Add egg mixture to sugar mixture; mix well. Pour batter into a greased 9" pie plate. Bake at 350 degrees for 30 minutes. Cut into wedges; serve warm or cooled. Serves 8.

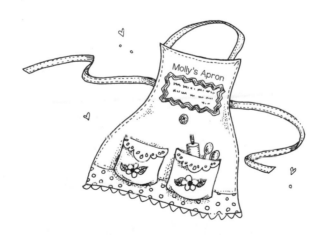

Baking together is a fun family activity and a great choice for kids just starting to learn how to cook. As you measure, mix and bake together, be sure to share any stories about hand-me-down cake or cookie recipes...you'll be creating memories as well as sweet treats!

Zesty Lemon Cheese Bars

Lisa Barger
Conroe, TX

*This recipe comes from a very old cookbook that I've had for years.
I added the lemon zest to give it a nice lemony kick!*

18-1/4 oz. pkg. lemon cake mix
2 eggs
1/3 c. oil
8-oz. pkg. cream cheese,
    softened

1/3 c. sugar
1 T. lemon juice
zest of 1 lemon

In a large bowl, combine dry cake mix, one beaten egg and oil; mix until crumbly. Reserve one cup crumb mixture for topping. Pat remaining mixture into an ungreased 13"x9" baking pan. Bake at 350 degrees for 15 minutes. In another bowl, beat cream cheese, sugar, lemon juice, lemon zest and remaining egg until light and smooth. Spread over baked layer. Sprinkle with reserved crumb mixture; bake 15 minutes longer. Cool; cut into bars. Makes 2 dozen.

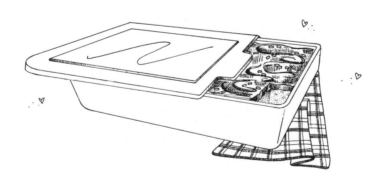

If you see a vintage cake pan with its own slide-on lid at a tag sale, snap it up! It's indispensable for toting cakes and cookies to potlucks and get-togethers.

Shareable
Desserts & Cookies

Shortcut Key Lime Pie

Pamela Myers
Auburn, IN

I tried this pie at a friend's birthday party. It was so delicious, I just had to have the recipe, although I wasn't looking forward to squeezing all of the limes! When I found out only one lime was squeezed, I knew this was a keeper. So easy and delicious!

1 whole lime
6-oz. can frozen limeade
   concentrate, thawed
14-oz. can sweetened
   condensed milk

1 c. sour cream
8-oz. container frozen whipped
   topping, thawed
9-inch graham cracker crust

Grate zest from lime; squeeze juice from lime. Slice lime; set aside. In a large bowl, mix limeade concentrate, condensed milk, sour cream and reserved lime juice until combined. Fold in whipped topping. Pour into pie crust; cover and refrigerate for 3 to 4 hours. Cut into wedges; garnish each with a slice of lime and a sprinkle of lime zest. Makes 8 servings.

Invite family & friends for a pie social! Everyone
brings their favorite pie...you provide the
ice cream and whipped topping.

Butterscotch Pinwheel Date Cookies

Arlene Smulski
Lyons, IL

A soft cookie full of rich butterscotch flavor, nuts and dates. It is a tasty change of pace from chocolate or vanilla-based cookies.

8-oz. pkg. pitted dates,
  finely chopped
1/2 c. water
1/3 c. sugar
1/2 c. pecan chips
1 c. butter, softened
2 eggs, beaten

1-3/4 c. light brown sugar,
  packed
1 t. baking soda
1/2 t. salt
3-1/2 c. all-purpose flour
1 t. vanilla extract

In a saucepan over low heat, combine dates, water, sugar and pecans; cook until thick. Remove from heat; set aside to cool. Meanwhile, mix remaining ingredients in a large bowl until evenly blended and smooth. Divide into 2 parts; roll out one part 1/4-inch thick between 2 sheets of wax paper. Spread half of date mixture over dough; roll up cinnamon roll-style. Repeat with remaining dough and date mixture. Chill for 2 hours or overnight. Slice rolls 1/4-inch thick; arrange on parchment paper-lined baking sheets. Bake at 350 degrees for 20 minutes, or until golden. Cool on a wire rack. Makes about 4 dozen.

Homebaked goodies are always a welcome gift. For a fun and frugal presentation, run brightly colored leftover wrapping paper through a paper shredder. Use it to fill a gift bag and tuck in a stack of wrapped cookies.

Shareable
Desserts & Cookies

Sally's Oven Caramel Corn

Norma Burton
Kuna, ID

This caramel corn has been a hit with family, friends and neighbors for years. My mother-in-law was a good cook and I got this recipe from her, along with many others. From autumn to Christmas, it is in demand at our house.

16 c. popped corn
1 c. butter, sliced
2 c. brown sugar, packed
1/2 c. light corn syrup

1 t. salt
1/2 t. baking soda
1 t. vanilla extract

Divide popcorn into 2 roasting pans or other large baking pans; remove any unpopped kernels and set aside. In a large saucepan, combine butter, brown sugar, corn syrup and salt. Bring to a boil over medium heat; boil for 5 minutes. Remove from heat; stir in baking soda and vanilla. Pour evenly over popped corn; stir to coat. Bake, uncovered, at 225 degrees for one hour, stirring every 15 minutes. Turn caramel corn out onto buttered baking sheets; allow to cool. Break apart; store in a tightly covered container. Makes about 16 cups.

Remember the fun of digging down in a box of caramel corn for the little prize? Make some homemade caramel corn and pack it up in individual take-out cartons. Wrap little toys and treasures in wax paper and hide 'em in the cartons for "remember when" giggles!

Ricotta Cake with Lemon Glaze

Jean DePerna
Fairport, NY

A light, very moist cake with a wonderful lemon flavor.
We like to garnish it with thin slices of lemons and sugared
fresh cranberries...looks so festive!

3/4 c. butter, room temperature
1-1/2 c. sugar
15-oz. container whole-milk
   ricotta cheese
3 eggs
1/2 t. vanilla extract

3/4 t. lemon extract
zest of 1 lemon
1-1/2 c. all-purpose flour
2 t. baking powder
1/2 t. baking soda
1/2 t. salt

In a large bowl, beat together butter and sugar with an electric mixer on medium-high speed until light and fluffy. Add ricotta cheese and blend well. Add eggs, one at a time, beating well after each. Add extracts and zest; mix well and set aside. In a separate bowl, sift together remaining ingredients. Add flour mixture to butter mixture in 2 parts, stirring just until blended. Pour batter into a buttered and floured Bundt® pan; smooth the top of batter. Bake at 350 degrees for 35 to 40 minutes, until a toothpick comes out clean. Let cool in pan for at least 15 minutes. Turn out cake onto a wire rack and cool completely. Drizzle Lemon Glaze over cake; let glaze set for 30 minutes. Cut into wedges and serve. Makes 10 servings.

Lemon Glaze:

2 c. powdered sugar
3 T. lemon juice

zest of 1 lemon

Whisk together all ingredients until thick and smooth.

Shareable
Desserts & Cookies

Apple Crunch Pizza

Jenita Davison
La Plata, MO

*I like to make my own homemade apple pie filling. One day, when
one jar didn't seal, I started looking for another way to use it.
I found an idea and came up with this tasty and fun recipe.*

21-oz. can apple pie filling
1/2 c. all-purpose flour
1/3 c. quick-cooking oats,
   uncooked
1/3 c. dark brown sugar, packed
1 t. cinnamon
1/4 c. butter, softened
Garnish: ice cream

Make No-Roll Pie Crust; spoon pie filling over crust and set aside. In a
bowl, mix together flour, oats, brown sugar and cinnamon; cut in butter.
Sprinkle over pie filling. Bake at 350 degrees for 40 to 45 minutes.
Place under the broiler for a short time to caramelize the topping. Cut
into wedges; serve with ice cream. Makes 12 servings.

No-Roll Pie Crust :

1-1/2 c. all-purpose flour
2 t. sugar
1 t. salt
1/2 c. oil
2 T. milk

Mix all ingredients well. Press into a 12" round pizza pan.

Serve up a bucket o' bones at your next Halloween party!
Press a mini marshmallow into each end of a pretzel stick
and dip in melted white chocolate.

Uncle Donald's Peanut Butter Cookies

Phyllis Ridenour
Bellflower, CA

This recipe goes back to my childhood, when I made these cookies every year for my Uncle Donald's birthday. He loved peanut butter cookies and he said these were the best! I've been making them for 50 years and still get requests for them all the time. I always think of my uncle with fond memories when I make them.

1 c. butter
1 c. creamy peanut butter
1 c. brown sugar, packed
1 c. sugar
2 eggs, beaten

1 t. vanilla extract
2-1/2 c. all-purpose flour
1 t. baking soda
1/2 t. salt

In a large bowl, stir together butter and peanut butter until blended. Add sugars and mix well. Add eggs and vanilla; mix well and set aside. In another bowl, mix remaining ingredients; add to butter mixture and mix well. Drop dough by large tablespoonfuls onto ungreased baking sheets. Dip a fork in cold water and make criss-cross marks on each cookie. Bake at 350 degrees for about 10 minutes. Cool on a wire rack. Makes about 3 dozen.

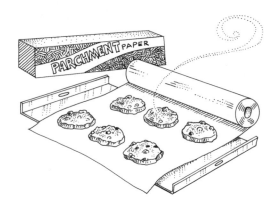

Parchment paper is a baker's best friend! Place it on a baking sheet to keep cookies from spreading and sticking. Clean-up is a breeze too. The paper can be usually be used again at least once...when it starts to darken, toss it.

Shareable
Desserts & Cookies

Yummy Peanut Butter Squares

Scarlett Hedden
Titusville, FL

Every time I make this easy no-bake recipe, I have to make sure I have extra copies of the recipe with me to give out. It is definitely delicious!

1-1/2 c. honey graham cracker crumbs
16-oz. pkg. powdered sugar
1-3/4 c. creamy peanut butter, divided

1 c. butter, melted
12-oz. pkg. semi-sweet chocolate chips

Add graham cracker crumbs to a large bowl. Add powdered sugar and 1-1/2 cups peanut butter; mix well. Blend in melted butter until well combined. Press mixture evenly into an ungreased 13"x9" baking pan; set aside. In a microwave-safe bowl, combine chocolate chips and remaining peanut butter. Melt in microwave for one minute on high; stir after one minute. Spread over crumb mixture in pan. Cover and chill for about 30 minutes, until just set. Cut into bars or bite-size squares. Makes 2 to 3 dozen.

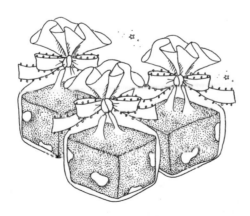

Wrap candies and cookies individually in squares
of colored cellophane. Handy treats to give as
party favors or to co-workers!

Justin's Amazing Chocolate Cake

Diane Bertosa
Brunswick Hills, OH

This chocolate cake is super-moist and delicious! It is the only cake my grandson Justin can eat because of his food allergies, and it's amazing because it contains no dairy products. Everyone in the family loves this special cake. We frost it with a dairy-free canned vanilla frosting.

3 c. all-purpose flour
2 c. sugar
6 T. baking cocoa
2 t. baking powder
2 t. baking soda
2/3 c. oil

2 c. water
2 T. white vinegar
1 T. vanilla extract
1/2 t. salt
Garnish: favorite frosting

In a large bowl, combine flour, sugar, cocoa, baking powder and baking soda; mix thoroughly and set side. In a separate bowl, combine remaining ingredients except garnish; mix well. Add to flour mixture; beat well until smooth. Batter will be very thin. Pour batter into a greased 13"x9" baking pan. Bake at 350 degrees for 25 to 30 minutes, using a toothpick to check for doneness. Cool; spread with frosting and cut into squares. Makes 12 servings.

Dust powdered sugar through a doily for a pretty yet simple cake decoration...check craft stores for seasonal stencils too!

Shareable
Desserts & Cookies

Special Snickerdoodles

Peggy Ann Hegelein
Binghamton, NY

A cookie jar classic! I discovered that adding a dash or two of nutmeg in these cookies gives them a unique flavor.

1/2 c. butter
1-1/4 c. sugar, divided
1/4 t. baking soda
1/4 t. cream of tartar
1/8 t. nutmeg

1 egg, beaten
1/2 t. vanilla extract
1-1/2 c. all-purpose flour
1-1/2 t. cinnamon

In a large bowl, beat butter with an electric mixer on medium speed for 30 seconds. Add one cup sugar, baking soda, cream of tartar, nutmeg, egg and vanilla; beat until combined. Beat in as much flour as possible; stir in remaining flour. Cover and chill for one hour. Combine cinnamon and remaining sugar in a small bowl. Shape dough into one-inch balls; roll in cinnamon-sugar. Arrange on ungreased baking sheets. Bake at 375 degrees for 10 minutes, or until edges are golden. Makes 3 dozen.

Stir up some Grizzly Gorp for snacking and tucking into lunchboxes. Just toss together 2 cups bear-shaped graham crackers, one cup mini marshmallows, one cup peanuts and 1/2 cup dried cranberries or raisins. Yum!

Autumn Gold Pumpkin Spice Cake

Linda Murray
Brentwood, NH

I have been making this delicious two-layer cake for years. It's become the traditional birthday cake for my daughter Linda, whose birthday is in November. When I sell it at American Legion bingo, it always sells out.

18-1/2 oz. pkg. yellow cake mix
3 eggs, beaten
1 c. water
1 c. canned pumpkin

1 t. cinnamon
1/4 t. nutmeg
1/4 t. ground ginger
Garnish: 1 c. chopped walnuts

In a large bowl, combine dry cake mix and remaining ingredients except garnish. Beat with an electric mixer on medium speed for 4 minutes. Divide batter into 2 greased and floured 8" round cake pans. Bake at 375 degrees for 30 to 35 minutes, until a toothpick inserted in center comes out clean. Set pans on a wire rack to cool; turn out of pans. Assemble layers with Frosting; spread frosting over cake. Decorate with chopped walnuts. Makes 10 to 15 servings.

Frosting:

16-oz. pkg. powdered sugar
1/2 c. shortening
1/2 t. cinnamon

1 t. vanilla extract
3 T. milk

Combine all ingredients in a large bowl. Beat with an electric mixer on medium speed until smooth, adding a little more milk for spreading consistency, if needed.

A party without cake is really just a meeting.
–Julia Child

Shareable
Desserts & Cookies

Chocolate-Caramel Crispy Bars   *Betty Lou Wright*
Fort Worth, TX

Don't shy away from the time it takes to unwrap a bag of caramels....
this delicious treat is well worth it! I've made this for years and it
continues to get rave reviews from family & friends. It's quite a
sweet-tooth pleaser!

5 c. crispy rice cereal
Optional: 1 c. peanuts
14-oz. pkg caramels, unwrapped
3 T. water

6-oz. pkg. semi-sweet
  chocolate chips
6-oz. pkg. butterscotch chips

Put cereal in a large bowl; add peanuts, if using, and set aside. Combine caramels and water in a saucepan over low heat. Cook, stirring often, until caramels are melted and mixture is smooth. Pour melted caramels over cereal; toss until well coated. With buttered fingers, press mixture into a greased 13"x9" baking pan. Sprinkle chocolate and butterscotch chips on top. Bake at 200 degrees for 5 minutes, or until chips soften. Use a table knife to spread softened chips until blended, to form a frosting. Cool; cut into bars. Makes 2 to 3 dozen.

Slice bar cookies into one-inch squares and set them
in frilly paper candy cups. Guests will love sampling
"just a bite" of several different treats.

215

Grandma Kendall's Welsh Cookies

Sally Hines
Old Forge, PA

My grandma, who was Welsh, used to have me watch her when she made these, because you learn by watching. I am thankful that she wrote it down for me before she passed away. Thank you, Grandma!

1 c. raisins	2 T. baking powder
1/2 c. hot water	1-1/2 t. cinnamon
6 c. all-purpose flour	1-1/2 t. nutmeg
1 c. lard	1 t. salt
1 c. butter, sliced	1 t. vanilla extract
3-1/4 c. sugar	small amount milk
4 eggs, beaten	

In a small bowl, combine raisins and hot water; set aside for a few minutes. In a large bowl, combine remaining ingredients except milk. Mix with your hands until dough forms, adding milk little by little as needed. Drain raisins and fold in. Cover and chill until firm. When ready to bake, roll out half of the dough on a floured surface, about 1/4-inch thick. Cut dough into rounds, using a 3" glass tumbler or biscuit cutter. Preheat an ungreased electric griddle to 350 degrees. Add cookies, a few at a time; cook until lightly golden on one side. Flip over only once and cook other side until golden. Repeat with remaining dough. Makes about 2 dozen.

Sprinkle powdered sugar on the work surface when rolling out cookie dough. So much tastier than using flour and it works just as well.

Shareable
Desserts & Cookies

Cranberry Upside-Down Muffins *Carolyn Deckard*
Bedford, IN

*I found this recipe several years ago in my husband's
mom's old recipe box. It brings back fond memories
every time I make them.*

3/4 c. whole-berry
    cranberry sauce
1/4 c. brown sugar, packed
2 c. all-purpose flour
2 T. sugar
1 T. baking powder

1/2 t. salt
1 c. skim milk
1/4 c. oil
2 egg whites, beaten
1 t. orange zest

Spray 12 muffin cups with non-stick vegetable spray. Spoon one
tablespoon cranberry sauce into each cup. Top each with one teaspoon
brown sugar; set aside. In a bowl, combine flour, sugar, baking powder
and salt; mix well and set aside. In a separate large bowl, combine
remaining ingredients; blend well. Add flour mixture to milk mixture,
all at once; stir just until moistened. Divide batter evenly over cranberries
and brown sugar in muffin cups. Bake at 400 degrees for 14 to
18 minutes, until a toothpick inserted in the center comes out clean.
Cool in pan for one minute. Run a table knife around edges of cups
to loosen. Invert muffins onto a wire rack set over wax paper; remove
pan. Cool for 5 minutes; serve warm. Makes one dozen.

For muffins that look bakery-perfect, sprinkle with
coarse sugar just before baking.

INDEX

INDEX

INDEX

Find Gooseberry Patch
wherever you are!

www.gooseberrypatch.com

Call us toll-free at 1·800·854·6673

homecoming parades colorful leaves

casual get-togethers

drives in the country

moonlit hayrides

craft fairs

 crackling bonfires community suppers

U.S. to Metric Recipe Equivalents

Volume Measurements

1/4 teaspoon	1 mL
1/2 teaspoon	2 mL
1 teaspoon	5 mL
1 tablespoon = 3 teaspoons	15 mL
2 tablespoons = 1 fluid ounce	30 mL
1/4 cup	60 mL
1/3 cup	75 mL
1/2 cup = 4 fluid ounces	125 mL
1 cup = 8 fluid ounces	250 mL
2 cups = 1 pint =16 fluid ounces	500 mL
4 cups = 1 quart	1 L

Weights

1 ounce	30 g
4 ounces	120 g
8 ounces	225 g
16 ounces = 1 pound	450 g

Oven Temperatures

300° F	150° C
325° F	160° C
350° F	180° C
375° F	190° C
400° F	200° C
450° F	230° C

Baking Pan Sizes

Square		Loaf	
8x8x2 inches	2 L = 20x20x5 cm	9x5x3 inches	2 L = 23x13x7 cm
9x9x2 inches	2.5 L = 23x23x5 cm	Round	
Rectangular		8x1-1/2 inches	1.2 L = 20x4 cm
13x9x2 inches	3.5 L = 33x23x5 cm	9x1-1/2 inches	1.5 L = 23x4 cm